BRAT PACK: CONFIDENTIAL

Andrew Pulver

Steven Paul Davies

B T Batsford • London

A catalogue record for this book is available from
the British Library.

ISBN 0 7134 8685 6

Printed in Frome, Somerset, Great Britain
by Butler and Tanner

Grateful acknowledgement to the Joel Finler
Collection for the supply of pictures.

Volume © B T Batsford 2000

First published in 2000 by
B T Batsford
9 Blenheim Court
Brewery Road
London N7 9NT

A member of the Chrysalis Group plc

Acknowledgements

Steven Paul Davies and Andrew Pulver would like to
thank Mark Connolly, Chris Chenery,
John Lewis Carlino, Alex Cox, Tod Davies,
Mike Figgis, Bill Fishman and
Teresa Howes, Jeremy Theobald, Tony Mancini and
Mary Morrison.

Contents

Introduction   4
A Golden Age   8
    by Andrew Pulver

The Films   12
    by Andrew Pulver

1983 – "When I stepped out into the bright sunlight"   12
1984 – "That's why they call them crushes"   24
1985 – "We think you're crazy"   31
1986 – "I'm so humiliated"   44
1987 – "You did it to yourself"   54
And After?   62
The New Teen Generation   69

The Players   74
    by Steven Paul Davies

Matthew Broderick   74   The Second Team   123
Tom Cruise   77
Matt Dillon   80   Kevin Bacon   123
Robert Downey Jr   83   Jon Cryer   125
Emilio Estevez   87   John Cusack   126
Anthony Michael Hall   91   Jami Gertz   129
Rob Lowe   94   Jennifer Grey   131
Ralph Macchio   97   C Thomas Howell   133
Andrew McCarthy   99   Timothy Hutton   135
Demi Moore   101   Mary Stuart Masterson   138
Molly Ringwald   104   Tim Robbins   140
Judd Nelson   106   Mickey Rourke   143
Sean Penn   109   James Spader   146
Ally Sheedy   113   Eric Stoltz   149
Charlie Sheen   116   Patrick Swayze   152
Kiefer Sutherland   119   Daphne Zuniga   155
Mare Winningham   121

Index   158

Introduction

by Andrew Pulver

What, in the end, are celebrities for? Different eras have different uses for them. It didn't seem so strange, in the mid-1980s, that a bunch of well-heeled, well-connected and well-rewarded young men and women should embody all that the decade stood for. They were movie actors, sure – but they had fast times on screen and off; and in their sleek self-regard they delivered the *coup de grâce* to the idea that the movies were an adult craft, the pursuit of the insane drug-addled genius or the philosophy-spouting shut-in. No, in the 1980s, the movies became the rumpus room for the undertalented and the overblown, the good-looking and the bad-behaving. Welcome to the world of the Brat Pack.

In the 1960s, a bunch of Hollywooders smoked and drank and canoodled their off-screen lives into public attention. They were the Rat Pack: Frankie, Dino, Joey, Sammy and the rest were the mocking counterparts to the button-down office roués that festooned Billy Wilder films like *The Seven Year Itch* or *The Apartment*. (Wilder even had Dean Martin turn up in person to torment one such hapless example, Orville J Spooner, in the movie *Kiss Me Stupid*.)

Two decades later, things had changed. After the Summer of Love and the punk upheaval, the movies' social demographic had jolted downwards by 20 years or so, and as the 1980s dawned there were teens running around all over the planet with hard currency in their pocket and not a whole lot – cinematically speaking – to spend it on. Enter the Brat Pack. From the outside, they looked like a group as internally coherent as the Rats – incestuous, vain, hedonist and spoilt beyond belief. A goodly proportion of them enjoyed a head start in the movie business, being the sons and daughters of powerful Hollywood figures. Others infiltrated the scene via television shows and working the audition circuit. Add on the letter 'B', and you had yourselves a new Pack.

The Brat Pack weren't the best actors of their generation, nor did they make the best movies, but in some indefinable way they distilled the spirit of their age and earned an ambiguous, collective place in the hearts of the hormone-racked adolescents who voraciously sucked down one movie after another. From our 21st-century vantage point, a decade and a half later, even the most enduring of the Brat Pack products seem clumsily scripted and ineptly put together – much like the music videos of similar vintage – but it's impossible to overestimate the emotional charge that much of their work carried for the serried ranks of teenagers who saw themselves, heightened and idealised maybe, flashing across the screen.

The Brat Pack movies told all kinds of stories, some of them simple, some of them ridiculous, some moving, some nausea-inducing. Not all of them were teen movies, for as the Pack got older, their movies did too, and had them tickling around the issues that beset young adults. Not every teen movie was a Brat Pack movie; there were stars and talents working outside the gilded sphere of privilege, who made their

(Opposite) The way they were . . . Rob Lowe, Demi Moore, Emilio Estevez, Mare Winningham, Judd Nelson, Ally Sheedy and Andrew McCarthy in a cast photograph of *St. Elmo's Fire.*

own contribution to a fondly remembered genre. Still, teen tales of resentment, self-loathing and wide-eyed gratification form the staple of the Brat Pack oeuvre, and, although the combination always changed, they were all linked by the unrelenting gang-mentality arrogance that the Brats brought with them. Like the cool kids in class, they didn't let just *anybody* be part of their scene – a movie, the audience, *you*, were damn lucky to be getting a look-in.

The intervening years have only added to the Brat Pack's lustre. The kids who slavishly watched the movies – say you were 15 in 1983 – grew up into the world-weary, ultra-knowing Generation X, a do-nothing generation that cherished and treasured its own formative experiences with a fervour and self-regard that's become almost embarrassing. And where did this self-regard come from? The Brats themselves set the example, feeding and inspiring as many teen demons as they appeared to exorcise. Appropriately enough, the Brat Pack have all gone their separate ways: some have become huge stars, others workaday actors; yet others are nursing career revivals and negotiating parole conditions. But once upon a time, they were all together, revelling in the limitless possibilities and awesome potential that lay ahead.

The acknowledged high point of the Brat Pack was the summer of 1985. *The Breakfast Club* was out and *St Elmo's Fire* in the can. In June, *New York* magazine ran a story identifying for the first time the existence of a new generation of Hollywood players. Rob Lowe, Judd Nelson and Emilio Estevez graced the cover picture, radiating whatever energy it took to *par-tay* all night. Writer David Blum characterised the threesome living life to the limit at LA's Hard Rock Café, chugging Coronas and magnetising the ladies. With the benefit of hindsight, some of Blum's assertions make interesting reading. He describes Emilio Estevez as the Brat Pack's unofficial president. He assures readers that Estevez's career as a major writer–director is only a matter of time. Molly Ringwald doesn't get a single mention. Harry Dean Stanton is name-checked as the Brat Pack's spiritual father. And, according to Blum, the movie that changed Hollywood, that brought the Brat Pack together… is *Taps*.

Now that the heyday of the Brat Pack is past, some readjustment is in order. First off: who, precisely, are the Brat Pack? Most would agree that Estevez, Ringwald, Lowe and Nelson beyond doubt exemplify the Brat Pack, but what defines their membership? And what about awesomely Bratty talents like Sean Penn, who by and large swerved by the teen movie cycle that is somehow central to the Brat Pack oeuvre? What, exactly, defines a Brat Pack movie anyway? These are hard questions to answer, but we will try.

As is the way of history, it takes time for coincidence to become a phenomenon. The heart and soul of the Brat Pack, in retrospect, were a gang of nine: the principal casts of two movies, *The Breakfast Club* and *St Elmo's Fire*, both released in 1985. They are as follows: Emilio Estevez, Andrew McCarthy, Robert Hepler Lowe, Demetria Gene Guynes (we know her better as Demi Moore, the surname taken from her first husband Freddie), Judd Nelson, Mary Megan Winningham, Molly Ringwald, Michael Anthony Hall (he swapped his first two names) and Alexandra Elizabeth Sheedy.

For this plucky ninesome, the Brat Pack movies remain their finest hour, the route through which the cinema-going public remember and identify them. There's one exception, of course: the redoubtable Demi Moore, who fought her way clear of the Brat Pack through dogged career choices and regular participation in successful mainstream movies throughout the late 80s and early 90s. In the same way, the smell of the Brat Pack has infected a fistful of other performers – some unbelievably famous, some missing in action – who came to prominence in the same rush of movie-goers enthusiasm. Where would Tom Cruise be without *The Outsiders*? Or Ralph Macchio and Matt Dillon, for that matter? Charlie Sheen took on the mantle of the Brat Pack even though his best 80s work was for Oliver Stone, the least Bratty director you could imagine. Like Charlie, Keifer Sutherland and Robert Downey Jr were *family*; connections helped you get into the Brat Pack, behaving like a maniac wasn't enough on its own.

The case of Timothy Hutton, hailed by David Blum as the original Brat Packer, is illuminating. In 1985, he would no doubt have appeared the archetype of the brooding teen performer, what with his Oscar for *Ordinary People* in 1980. But a longer view reveals that Hutton's career as a teen idol was pretty much over by 1982, after the debacle of *Turk 182!*, making him a far-from-central figure in Brat Pack lore. It's also for this reason that *Taps*, the 1981 film that united him, Tom Cruise and Sean Penn, can't seriously remain a landmark Brat Pack film. That honour, self-evidently, must go to *The Outsiders*, made two years later, which was the occasion that the Brat Pack as we know it took on coherent form, bringing Cruise, Estevez, Lowe and Matt Dillon onto the same piece of celluloid. The double centre of the Brat Pack web, *The Breakfast Club* and *St Elmo's Fire,* embody the two contrasting strains that repeat themselves throughout the Brat Pack body of work. On the one hand, we have John Hughes, we have sensitivity, we have emotions; on the other, we have Joel Schumacher, we have flash, we have self-indulgence. By 1988, it was all over: the Brats had grown up or gone away, the kids had – like all kids before and since – turned against what they had once adored.

What follows in this first section is an analysis of the key components of Brat Pack cinema. It is by no means a comprehensive account, for there are moments of mid-80s cinematic insanity that deserve to lie undisturbed in whatever foul corner they have fetched up. But the movies that shaped the Brat Pack are examined in detail, year by year, as they defined the youth movies of the era. Also appended is a short account of the teen cinema revival of the late 90s, which provides an illuminating study in how movies are shaped and controlled in our own generation, and how they contrast with the earlier films. The second section of this book offers biographical accounts of each individual performer, how they earned their reputation and won their spurs.

A Golden Age

Where did the Brat Pack come from? What irresistible social force allowed it to come into being? The teen movie was one of the 1980s great phenomena: undervalued at the time by both the film industry and film critics, but now the subject of much fond after-the-event recall. Audiences of the time have maintained their appreciation as they chug into their third decade. They've fought their hormonal battles, licked the wounds and are now ready for some rest and recreation. And what better way to reminisce than the cinematic manuals that helped them through their most troubled, darkest times?

What's become apparent, years later, is that appreciation of the 80s teen movies reflects that of the teens themselves – grown-ups just didn't understand them. But why did this outpouring of emotion wait until the 1980s to well up and explode, like a pustule on an adolescent nose? Teens had been around, as a socially and economically identifiable force, since the 1950s. They had their own icons in James Dean and Marlon Brando, Tuesday Weld and Natalie Wood. And they had their own movies: from *The Wild One* and *Rebel Without a Cause* in the mid-1950s to *Beach Blanket Bingo* and *Muscle Beach Party* in the mid-1960s, teens could thrill to the alternate impulses of sassing old-timers and oiling their glistening pecs in the surf.

Those movies served their function – as date-night fodder and vague expressions of adolescent discontent. But they hardly addressed the *issues* – or if they did, they did it in a humourless, heavy-handed way. But how could they? They were films made either by mom and pop or by that weird guy hanging around on the corner with a bunch of nudie-cutie postcards in his jacket pocket. In other words, by the old-timers themselves, inside a dictatorial studio system that kept them all in work, or by low-rent exploitation merchants like Roger Corman turning out cheap movies as fast as humanly possible.

Ironically, when all this came to an end in the late 1960s as the Hollywood new wave rushed the gates of the palace, it signalled an end to what few reasons there might have been for the curious teen to haunt the movie theatre. Although Hollywood's 70s generation undeniably initiated a golden age, they did it by making *adult* films. And not pornography either, although to audiences of the time there was occasional confusion. The era that brought us *M.A.S.H.*, *The Godfather* and *Bonnie and Clyde* also spawned *Deep Throat*, *The Story of O* and *Emmanuelle*. In its post-hippie, after-the-party mood, cinema was determined to bring all sacred cows crashing down. The American directors of the time – Coppola, Scorsese, Bogdanovich – were called Brats too: Movie Brats. Their movies nailed the concerns of a jittery, disillusioned America, with both Vietnam and Watergate on its conscience; but the golden age of the movie brats couldn't last. How could it? They didn't make movies for teens.

Those who did – George Lucas and Steven Spielberg – changed the face of the industry yet again in the mid-1970s. *Jaws* and *Star Wars* hauled in the kind of young audiences who were largely alienated by the Movie Brats' later efforts, and Hollywood faced the tough truth that artistic fertility had coincided with economic downturn. It emerged from the

1970s knowing that teens were at least part of the answer to its problems. Years before *Star Wars*, however, George Lucas had pointed the way. If ever a film-maker had his finger on the pulse, it was Lucas. His second feature *American Graffiti*, released in 1973, was a bittersweet memoir of his own high-school days in Modesto 10 years earlier. The big thing, though, about *American Graffiti* was it took $115m, on an investment of $750,000. One sweet deal.

Another step in the evolutionary ladder was taken five years later with *National Lampoon's Animal House*, directed by John Landis. Like *American Graffiti*, it was set in 1962, and it was motivated largely by the pot-smoking, politically inflected satire of the *Saturday Night Live* school. Fortunately, though, it contained a parade of idiotic frat-house antics that have since become legion, to be repeated in endless variation in one campus-set movie after another throughout the 1980s. Most important was the $141m it took in box office receipts, making it the most successful film comedy released to that date.

The final, irrevocable step was taken in 1981. A low-budget Canadian movie, *Porky's*, came out of nowhere to score another $100m-plus box-office take in America's cinemas. This was serious. *Porky's* had no pretensions to bittersweet nostalgia, nor left-field political satire. It was simply a story of a bunch of high-schoolers on a desperate quest for pleasures of the flesh. By contrast with what was to come later, *Porky's* remains engagingly rambling and relatively subtle in its deployment of low-key camerawork. But who remembers that now? The shower scene, the inflated condom, the howling schoolteacher – these are what ensured Porky's has passed into movie immortality. And it concentrated the minds of teenage audiences like never before. Teen movies, as the 1980s were to know them, had arrived. Like *Graffiti* and *Animal House*, *Porky's* is set in a more strait-laced America, in this case Florida, 1954. This time-shift is the crucial factor that endows all three movies with a parable-like quality. The agonies and frustrations of the teens at their centre are thrown into ever sharper relief for their audiences' agonised delectation. *Porky's*, however, showed that these frustrations alone were enough to make a successful movie, if you threw in enough dick and fart jokes to keep the entertainment level up.

At the same time, teens were getting sliced and diced in a rash of horror films, kicking off with *Halloween* in 1979. Technically, *Halloween* belongs to the Roger Corman school of independently made exploitation films, since John Carpenter and his team found non-studio finance to make it. But its legacy was immediate and is still being felt today. It also sprang from the same desire to give the teen audience what it wanted. *Halloween* was a nerve-shattering excuse for dating couples to grab on to each other in the movie house, even as the on-screen teens, wayward in their sexualised antics, were punished by the remorseless Michael Myers. Other teen-chomping franchises were quickly established, the most prominent being the *Friday the 13th* series (starting in 1980) and the *Nightmare on Elm Street* movies (beginning in 1984).

The new teen genre, however, soon showed it had a heart. Precocious music journalist Cameron Crowe, tired of being *Rolling Stone* magazine's fresh-faced prodigy, enrolled in a high school to write an undercover story. A book resulted, *Fast Times at Ridgemont High*, and soon a movie, released in 1982, which would establish the template for the heights of sophistication to which a teen movie could aspire. Jennifer Jason Leigh, Brian Backer, Phoebe Cates and Judge Reinhold illuminate a humane, sensitive study of high-schoolers bending under the weight of peer-group pressures – although Sean Penn, as surf rat Spicoli, supplies a genre-defining creation that leavens proceedings with top-quality stoner comedy. ("So what Jefferson was saying was: hey, you know, we left that England place because it was bogus. So if we don't get ourselves some cool rules ourselves, pronto, then we'll be bogus too.").

The Brat Pack itself was stirring into life at the same time. Before *Fast Times*, Penn appeared in *Taps*, a military academy movie directed by Harold Becker. It also saw a role for a youthful Tom Cruise in support of Timothy Hutton and George C Scott. *Taps* followed a bunch of cadets as they fought off property developers trying to take over their school. A precursor of the wave of military-academy movies of the early 80s (*An Officer and a Gentleman*, *The Lords of Discipline*), *Taps* is only tangentially a teen movie. Moreover, it doesn't *feel* like a Brat Pack movie, since none of the core Gang of Nine is anywhere to be found.

The first Brat Pack movie that we may consider official had to wait until 1983, when Francis Ford Coppola corralled a bunch of Hollywood's brightest young actors for his answer to *American Graffiti*. *The Outsiders* was another 60s-set tale of youth rebellion, and through its offices Rob Lowe, Tom Cruise, Emilio Estevez and C Thomas Howell all forced their way onto the Hollywood map. *The Outsiders* acted as the high point of a family tree, with its participants going on to make a flood of often-successful movies in each others' company over the next five years. The Brat Pack's apotheosis came in 1985, when two ensemble movies, *The Breakfast Club* and *St Elmo's Fire*, were released within months of each other, sharing cast members and a similar confidence in their distillation of the teen experience. The penny dropped; the label stuck. By 1988, the Brat Pack cycle was pretty much over: the key Brats had gone their separate ways. In the eternally 80s way, no one actually wanted to be identified with the label that made them famous.

The teen movie itself chugged on regardless: non-Brat movies like *The Sure Thing*, *Heathers* and *Say Anything...* ensured that the cycle perpetuated itself, kept the paying customers happy and provided a springboard for other young performers to take off into the Hollywood stratosphere. But the new teen stars – Winona Ryder, John Cusack, Christian Slater – grew up in their turn, and the teen movie as we know it began to crumble as the 1980s ended. *Heathers* (1990), in particular, delivered a *coup de grâce*: the high-school experience was characterised as an eternal cycle of viciousness and self-hate. No longer could the teen world be seen as a haven for the working-out of sensitive emotions or a bear-pit for a clash of developing personality.

In an unlikely twist of events, teen movies underwent a revival in the late 1990s. Setting the pace was the Alicia Silverstone vehicle *Clueless*, which turned *Heathers* on its head and made the rich kid an earnest, well-meaning love-spreader. In its wake has come a whole raft of teen movies, staffed by yet another generation of teen movie stars. Sarah Michelle Gellar, Freddie Prinze Jr, Jennifer Love Hewitt... these are among the beneficiaries of a movie phenomenon prompted, as much as anything, by the desire to find ways of exploiting the popularity of youth-oriented television shows. But it's a phenomenon that has yet to run its course, fuelled as much by misty-eyed nostalgia for the likes of *The Breakfast Club* and *Pretty in Pink* as by appreciation for the eternal teen-movie verities of whipcord-smart dialogue and shamelessly soppy romance.

All these movies, whatever their primary function, share a central factor: an unashamed and unaffected deployment of archetypes. The poster for *The Breakfast Club* memorably

shoved it right up front, enumerating its principals as "a brain, a beauty, a jock, a rebel, and a recluse". In their unswerving recycling of these basic units, teen movies often resemble the classic structure of primitive mythology. Ugly ducklings are everywhere, menacing ogres are there to be repulsed (as often by a shower of vomit as anything else). But teen movies are also instinctively sociological: located in strictly defined and controlled communities, they offer at their best a compelling and subtle analysis of a bewildering social network with a pecking order of its own. Teens themselves make the perfect models for this: old enough to recognise and filter social hierarchies, yet too young to rise above it.

It was in this framework that the Brat Pack were to make their movies: an unlikely conjunction of the rankest exploitation and the most tremulous of emotions. Uniquely among cinematic genres, the teen movie could veer from the most leering, bra-tearing eyeful to the most sickening of humiliations – often in the very next shot. The best of the teen movies possess a kind of freewheeling insanity that is as turbulent as its central characters' hormones. The 70s auteurs, who were blown out of the water by Hollywood's commercial revival in the latter half of the decade, may not have approved of what came after them, but in engineering the collapse of the old studio system they broke open Hollywood's floodgates for a kind of continuous revolution, a kind of never-ending panic that ensured that the teen movie could expend all its anarchic energy. And for that we should be grateful.

Don't you want me, baby . . .
Emilio Estevez and Ally Sheedy in
The Breakfast Club.

THE FILMS by Andrew Pulver

1983

"When I stepped out into the bright sunlight…"

The Outsiders

1983 was the year of the Hitler Diaries, Cabbage Patch dolls, the invasion of Grenada, TV-am, and 'Let's Dance'. It was also the year of the Brat Pack. Still reeling from the financial and critical body blow of his musical *One From the Heart*, Francis Ford Coppola sniffed something promising in a letter sent to him by a school librarian from Fresno. She advised him that her students all felt a movie adaptation of a novel by Susie Hinton – written in 1967, when she was 15 – called *The Outsiders* would be a fine idea, and that in their opinion he would be the ideal director. *The Outsiders* wasn't the first SE Hinton adaptation (*Tex*, starring Matt Dillon, had been released the year before), but Coppola started shooting in Tulsa, Oklahoma, in March 1982, employing the same primitive-but-pioneering electronic film-making techniques that had so disastrously been put to use on his previous film. Parked up in a gizmo-packed trailer nicknamed the 'Silver Fish', Coppola completed production on both *The Outsiders* and its companion-piece *Rumble Fish*, in a mere seven months.

Hinton's story concerned a bunch of Tulsa kids split by teen-tribe affiliation and social background. The 'greasers' are dirt-poor, dysfunctional and white trash; the 'socs' are high-tone, cardigan-and-slacks-wearing country clubbers. Hinton's basic purpose was to show kids running their own lives; her novel, setting a Brat Pack and teen-movie trend, describes a world where parental influence and authority is explicitly negligible and ineffective.

In rendering this epic of tumultuous adolescent emotions, Coppola's casting choices were epoch-making. The parentless Curtis brothers — Darrel, Ponyboy and Sodapop — were played by Patrick Swayze, C Thomas Howell and Rob Lowe. Ponyboy's best pal Johnny Cade was played by Ralph Macchio. Matt Dillon was lead greaser troublemaker Dallas Winston. Tom Cruise and Emilio Estevez oiled up their thatches as makeweight gang-members. Diane Lane and former shirt-open-to-the-navel 70s crooner Leif Garrett fleshed out the socs. With the exception of Garrett, Coppola's strike rate of stars-to-be was impressive. Before *The Outsiders*, this motley collection of bit-parters, television actors and nothing-movie leads was a random sampling of Hollywood flotsam; afterwards, we had ourselves a Brat Pack.

Rebel yell . . . Matt Dillon,
C Thomas Howell and Ralph
Macchio in *The Outsiders*.

Like *American Graffiti*, *Animal House* and *Porky's* before it, *The Outsiders* stepped back into an earlier era to service the self-absorbed emotional abandon demanded by 1980s teens. The movie's opening scene is set at a drive-in movie theatre – which just happens to be showing a double-bill of the mid-60s version of teen movies, *Beach Blanket Bingo* and *Muscle Beach Party*. This is shorthand, clearly, to show that *The Outsiders'* teens are ill-used and misunderstood by the society they live in. And no one is more misunderstood than Ponyboy Curtis, the greaser who dares to love. His target is that fox of a soc Cherry Vallance, whom he protects from hassle from the hands of his own pal Dallas; straightaway, the movie launches into its us-against-them, mid-west Romeo and Juliet love story.

Bad blood between the two sects simmers; it boils over when Ponyboy, driven out the house by his domineering elder brother Darrel, hooks up with greasy-but-sensitive Johnny and heads off into their night. A gang of socs catch up with them, and in the resulting rumble, Johnny pulls a switchblade and leaves one of the socs spilling his guts in a fountain.

Tough talk . . . Emilio Estevez, Matt Dillon and Ralph Macchio in *The Outsiders*.

Urged to head for the hills by Dallas, the pair hole up in an abandoned church – there to discover the eternal truths enshrined in Robert Frost's lubricious poem *Nothing Gold Can Stay*. (The phrase also gets a work-out in Stevie Wonder's hit title song.) Later in the movie, as he lies dying, Johnny Cade provides a neat synopsis of the sentiment that underpinned the pro-kid, anti-adult attitude of the classic teen movie. "When you're a kid," he mutters, "everything's new, dawn. Like the way you dig sunsets, Pony, that's gold. Keep it that way, it's a good way to be." Johnny sees clear, then dies. That's movies.

Johnny's terminal insights are actually caused when he, Ponyboy and a visiting Dallas rescue a bunch of kids from a burning school – thereby allowing them to redeem themselves and return home. A massive rumble between the greasers and socs then ensues, still impressive in this day and age for its muddy barbarity. The acres of drenched T-shirts and slimed-up muscle here confirm the intention that's been sneakingly present throughout the movie, that Coppola is focusing on the lithe, callow forms of his young cast. There's no prurience about *The Outsiders*, though: Coppola's motive appears to be a self-conscious celebration of youthful energy, with furrowed biceps as plentiful as furrowed brows.

But the key, template-setting theme of *The Outsiders* that reverberates through the whole Brat genre is simply its teen angst. From Cherry Vallance's artless appeal to Ponyboy ("If I see you in school and don't say hi, don't take it personal") to Johnny Cade's parent-hating whimper ("I can't take much more of this") *The Outsiders* is one long howl of impotent teen

rage and frustration, expertly dramatised by both Hinton and Coppola. Teen movies would never be the same again.

Rumble Fish, on the other hand, serves to illustrate why the Brat Pack and auteur directors don't really mix. Where *The Outsiders* is clear, simple, emotionally lucid and undeniably gripping, *Rumble Fish* is confusing, overelaborate and undeniably uninvolving. Coppola read *Rumble Fish*, another Susie Hinton novel, while shooting *The Outsiders*, asked Matt Dillon and Diane Lane to stick around, and went straight into production.

Unluckily for the mainstream teen audience, Coppola decided to push the aesthetic envelope all the way. The narrative is reduced to a cryptic, bare-bones shorthand. The cinematography, although impressive, operates in a harsh, shadowy netherworld that stunned art-movie freaks and commercials directors, and no one else. Most importantly, *Rumble Fish* had hardly any of the loveable emoters that teens loved; for sure, it had Matt Dillon in a ripped singlet and razor-sharp cheekbones, but could anyone *love* this guy?

If you dig beneath the muddy storytelling and the obfuscating camera angles, it's clear that *Rumble Fish* could have been perfect Brat Pack material. Dillon plays Rusty-James, a petty thug longing, *Quadrophenia*-style, for the kind of gang rumbles that would give meaning to his life. His elder brother, the Motorcycle Boy (Mickey Rourke), turns up to save the teenage hot-head from a slashing, and tries to put him off gangs by showing him Siamese fighting fish in a local pet shop: "These are rumble fish – they'd kill each other if they could."

Brothers in Arms . . . Matt Dillon and Mickey Rourke in *Rumble Fish*.

Do the hustle . . . Matt Dillon and
Mickey Rourke (opposite) and
Dillon (left) both in *Rumble Fish*.

Rumble Fish finishes the same way as *The Outsiders*, with a sacrificial death, as the Motorcycle Boy invites the local cops to shoot him. His self-immolation holds out a prospect of an escape from wastoid hell. "I want you to break the cycle," he tells Rusty-James. "I want you to leave. I want you to follow the river, find the ocean." After setting free the Siamese fighting fish in the river (and most likely setting off an ecological disaster of cataclysmic proportions), Rusty-James heads off and is last seen propping up his bike at the ocean's edge. He's succeeded where the Motorcycle Boy failed.

Like *The Outsiders*, *Rumble Fish* is a world where adults play only a compromised part (the boys' liquored-up father is played by Dennis Hopper as a deadbeat of caricatural proportions) and it's another howl of impotent frustration against a betraying society. But the Brat Pack, if nothing else, were creatures of the mainstream, and *Rumble Fish* is too arcane a cinematic experience to act as any kind of template. Coppola himself was no longer interested, anyway; his next movie was *The Cotton Club* and all the grief *that* entailed. But that's another story.

CK-NE-4

All in the family . . . Jacqueline
Bisset, Andrew McCarthy and
Rob Lowe (opposite), and Bisset
and Lowe (above) in *Class*.

Far more characteristic of what was to come is *Class*, which ran fast and hard away
from any of the aesthetic pretensions of the Coppola canon. It had a definitively
non-auteur director, Lewis John Carlino (a former scriptwriter whose previous
directorial efforts included an adaptation of Yukio Mishima's novel *The Sailor who Fell From
Grace With the Sea* – with Kris Kristofferson). It had two future Brat Packers, Andrew
McCarthy and Rob Lowe, in living colour. It's set in a time-frame and an environment
largely similar, and recognisable to, the one inhabited by its audience. And it was an
unashamed example of the spotty-adolescent-wish-fulfilment movie. How deeply do
you have to be dreaming to suggest that Jacqueline Bisset would want to get down and
dirty with Andrew McCarthy in a glass-panelled lift?

That's the pivotal, and most instantly memorable, incident of the movie, but
there would be little to elevate it over a throwaway stunt in a frat-house movie
if that was all there was to it. *Class* starts with Jonathan (McCarthy) checking in
to a top-notch private school, where his room-mate is the implausibly smooth-
skinned Skip (Lowe). Skip is the kind of person whose self-regard is so extreme
that he dresses himself as Jesus Christ for a costume party. After a selection of

Part time lovers . . . Jacqueline Bisset and Andrew McCarthy in *Class*.

introductory pranks (Jonathan is stranded in a packed school yard clad only in bra and panties; Skip is fooled into thinking his room-mate has killed himself), the pair bond. Skip does his best to help his new pal to pop his cherry, after Jonathan's nervousness with the ladies results in spraying vomit, ripped dresses and elderly acquaintances plastered in cream cakes ("Till you get laid, none of us are safe").

Alone and disconsolate, $50 in his pocket, Jonathan then heads off to Chicago where, in a bar called Free 'n' Easy, he hooks up with the fur-coated Bisset. An epic encounter, but one that turns nightmarish when Skip invites Jonathan to stay over the Christmas holidays (incidentally establishing another perennial teen movie theme – the guilt felt by the moneyed teen toward his less-well-off buddy). Jonathan meets the parents, and yes… Bisset is Skip's mother.

At this point, the knockabout bachelor party atmosphere dissipates and *Class* turns into an impressively miserable portrait of guilt, duplicity and the perils of growing up. Before he knows what's happening, Jonathan is in over his head: lying to Skip, hurting the thing he loves (Mrs Skip) and generally wishing he were a kid again. When honesty is forced on him, after Skip catches the loving couple in the sack, humiliation is the major result. Only after a huge, cathartic punch-up do Skip and Jonathan mend their differences; and, in yet another perennial teen movie theme, their applications to an Ivy League university are accepted.

After a heartrending scene in which she suffers the salacious inquisition of her son's friends when they find her in a hotel bedroom with Jonathan, Bisset's character is sadly underused and largely forgotten in *Class*'s parcel-post ending. If it's any compensation, *Class* marked the first screen appearance of John Cusack, who announces his presence with the words: "Great, douchebag."

The good son . . . Tom Cruise and Rebecca de Mornay in *Risky Business*.

* * * * *

Setting its mark, though, at the wish-fulfilment end of the teen movie spectrum is *Risky Business*. Released in July 1983, *Risky Business* was the last time that Tom Cruise willingly allowed himself contact with the teen scene, and it marked his final entry in the Brat Pack roster. With the ticket to stardom the movie represented, he lost no time in surrounding himself with top-line directorial talent (Martin Scorsese, Oliver Stone, Paul Newman, the Scotts Ridley and Tony) or expensive hardware. This boy was going places.

He was still nerdy enough for a teen movie in the early 80s, though. In *Risky Business*, he plays the classic 80s straight arrow Joel Goodson (is the surname symbolic *enough*, do you think?) with the twin obsessions of losin' it and getting into Princeton. His parents (exemplary non-listeners) go away for a few days; his fright-wigged pal Miles (Curtis Armstrong) encourages him with the mantra "what the fuck?"; and within hours Joel is on the phone arranging for a call-girl to visit. After a false start, up pops hard-as-nails ice

Who's gonna drive you home? . .
Tom Cruise and Porsche in *Risky
Business*.

maiden Lana (Rebecca De Mornay), whose professional sack-artistry rocks Joel's world.

Short of money to pay her, Joel heads off to the bank. On his return, Lana has disappeared, but so has his mother's precious glass egg. Like the good son he is, Joel embarks on a quest to retrieve it, a quest that results in him, Lana and Miles being chased by a gun-wielding pimp; his dad's Porsche winding up at the bottom of Lake Michigan; a gaggle of prostitutes staying at his family residence; and getting seriously behind in his schoolwork. To remedy/take advantage of all these situations, Joel and Lana have the bright idea of getting their two sets of friends together – horny high-schoolers and professional pleasure-givers – and scoring big bucks. It's at this point that Cruise dons the deadly Ray-Bans-and-cigarette combination, to show his transformation from school nerd to savvy hustler.

The rest is history. Joel gets into Princeton, retrieves his parents' furniture (Lana's pimp has purloined it) and makes out with Lana *on a train*. Where *Risky Business* scores is its explicit equation of hardball entrepreneurship and prostitution – all business people are whores, it tells us. And, in a characteristically 80s manner, that's not a moral judgment – it's just a fact of life. Wear your shades with pride.

* * * * *

Finally, 1983 saw the release of the hugely popular science-geek thriller *WarGames*. Although Matthew Broderick, its star, is far too likeable a performer ever fully to fit into the Brat Pack mould, *WarGames* gives us a first good look at one of the Pack's key personnel, Ally Sheedy. Stuck in the thankless role of girlfriend/hanger-on, Sheedy exudes a golden-girl charisma that showed she was marked out for better things.

WarGames, along with its far-less-popular relative *Tron*, encapsulated humankind's mistrust of the already-burgeoning computer age. Broderick plays David Lightman, an expert bedroom hacker who inadvertently grapples with the computer controlling the US missile defences when he accepts an online invitation to play a 'game' called Global Thermonuclear War. His girl Jennifer (Sheedy), always seen with spandex jogging gear performing some horrible gymnastic feat, is proof that David's not the dysfunctional shut-in some might automatically assume he'd have to be: if an outdoorsy, athletic girl like that can fall for him, there's hope for him yet.

As it turns out, the Army tracks down David after he scares them halfway to Mutually Assured Destruction; he escapes from their clutches by crawling through air vents in a manner the Cruiser would emulate in *Mission: Impossible*; and, along with Jennifer, hunts down the rogue scientist who controls the maverick microchip. Fabulous.

Electric dreams . . . Matthew Broderick and Ally Sheedy in *WarGames*.

1984

"That's why they call them crushes. If they were easy,
they'd call them something else."

Pretty in Pink

1984 was the year we were supposed to be attending the Two Minutes Hate,
yattering in Newspeak and doing our morning fitness routines in front of
the television. In reality, 1984 was the year of John Hughes. If Francis Ford
Coppola was the midwife to the Brat Pack, then John Hughes was its guru, its
father–confessor and its agony aunt all rolled into one. Hughes's directorial
debut, *Sixteen Candles*, was released in May of this year, the first in a loose trilogy
that represents his Brat Pack masterwork. Hughes had already made his mark as
a gag-writer for *National Lampoon* magazine, and impressed Hollywood with
screenplays both produced (*National Lampoon's Vacation*, *Mr Mom*) and
unproduced (*Jaws Three – People Zero*). He started directing movies on the back
of an extraordinarily rich creative streak – *The Breakfast Club* had already been
scripted before *Sixteen Candles* got off the ground, but as yet had no takers; *Pretty
in Pink* was written 'the week after' *Sixteen Candles* was finished, according to a
1986 interview with Hughes in *Seventeen* Magazine. Truly, a great year.

Like practically all Hughes movies, *Sixteen Candles* is set in the mythical burg
of Shermer, Illinois, a suburb of Chicago like Hughes's own hometown of
Northbrook. In fact, Chicago and its environs are the definitive landscape of the
teen movie – the Goodsons from *Risky Business* hail from there too, as does
Ferris Bueller and the families in *The Breakfast Club*.

Sixteen Candles also marked the first collaboration between Hughes and Brat
Packer extraordinaire Molly Ringwald. First seen in her bedroom waking up on
the morning of her 16th birthday, Samantha Baker (Ringwald) is disconsolate.
"You're 16 today," she mutters. "Physically, you're still 15. Hopeless." Longing
for the attributes of adulthood is, we quickly learn, Samantha's central activity.
"You need 4 inches of bod and a great birthday." Hence the shock, humiliation
and mortification that lies in store for her on this special day. Tragically, the
whole event has slipped her entire family's mind; they're bound up with her
older sister's impending wedding. Later, in school, a 'confidential' sex
questionnaire finds its way into the hands of the (good-looking and older) boy
she names in the who-you'd-do-it-with section. On the bus, a skinny geek puts
the moves on her. Back home, one set of grandparents take over her bedroom;
the other make hideously embarrassing remarks about her burgeoning chest
("they're so *perky!*"). Later still she's scared out of her wits by the sudden

appearance of a Chinese exchange student, who introduces himself with the immortal phrase – "What's happening, hot stuff?"

But *Sixteen Candles* is no mere catalogue of adolescent fumblings and embarrassments. In Hughes's hands, the movie becomes an exquisitely observed parable, in which adolescent confusions, aspirations and the search for identity are an emotional obstacle course almost beyond endurance. "I'm 16," Samantha moans. "Everything should be platinum. I should be happy. But I can't *get* happy. It's physically impossible." This is teendom as the long dark night of the soul.

Samantha's long dark night of the soul is an actual event – the school dance. No sooner has she got inside the door and "made herself available", than she locks eyes with the moody Jake, who's slow-dancing with his prom-queen girlfriend to the mordant strains of Spandau Ballet's *True*. (Hughes would go on to exploit the heartstring-tugging qualities of Anglo-pop's finest in subsequent movies). Jake, we've already learned, isn't a standard-issue sporto – he tells his jock pal that "Maybe I'm interested in more than a party." Across the immense gulf separating youth from adulthood, childishness from maturity, freshmen from seniors, a connection has been made.

It's at this moment of supreme soppiness that The Geek, aka Farmer Ted (Anthony Michael Hall) chooses to make his most resolute attempt to score with Samantha. Faced with his charmless gyrations, she can only flee in terror and mortification. Later, after he's firmed up a bet with his proto-computer-nerd friends (one of whom, inevitably, is a young John Cusack), he shows up in the metalshop, where Samantha is sitting miserably in a bisected car. So begins a scene that encapsulates all the contrary brilliance of Hughes and his Brat Packers. Ringwald exudes finger-twisting vulnerability as she is persuaded to explain why she's so hostile. In return for her decision to trust him, the Geek confesses to his virginity ("This information cannot leave this room, okay? It would devastate my reputation as a dude"). Then, with hormone-addled contrariness, he immediately attempts to clamber all over her. She pushes him off and tells him about Jake. *To impress her*, he serves up his rival on a plate, telling Samantha (truthfully) that Jake asked him about her. While she's still on Cloud Nine at the information, the Geek asks for and obtains her underwear to allow him to save face with his friends. Cut to the gents toilet: a strutting Geek holds the precious evidence in triumphal pose for the baying crowd of spotty kids.

One character reversal after another, equally hilarious and touching; in this 10-minute scene, the Brat Pack movie came of age. The rest of the film is a simple unspooling of the narrative lines and emotional themes raised here. Samantha's dark night finishes on the sofa at home, to where she's been evicted from her bedroom to sleep; it's there that she fully contemplates her loss of nerve at the dance ("it just hurts"). Jake, meanwhile, shuffles his girlfriend off on the Geek and races over to the Baker wedding in time to snare Samantha before she gives up on the male species forever.

Sixteen Candles is by no means perfect; the most obvious difficulty is the running ridicule of the Chinese student Long Duk Dong, who takes abuse alarmingly close to outright racism. (Those who assume that ethnic-stereotype comedy is inherently racist should see the Howard Cosell-imitating Korean boy racers in Savage Steve Holland's non-Brat teen romance *Better Off Dead*...) And although putting the make on drunken women was practically a stand-by in any frat-house comedy in the 80s, it looks frighteningly like date-rape in this day and age. Despite all that, *Sixteen Candles* remains a breakthrough in the depiction of teen anxieties, a movie completely at the eye level of its subjects.

* * * * *

Oxford Blues, in bold contrast, is a movie built to show off its star, and suffers for it. Movie-goers anxious for more of Rob Lowe after *Class* next saw him in the ensemble art movie *The Hotel New Hampshire,* where the presence of class acts like Tony 'Tom Jones' Richardson, Jodie Foster and John Irving effectively prevented the movie from gaining any consideration as to Brat Pack status. Unlike Tom Cruise, however, Lowe plunged straight back into the Pack with this remake of *A Yank at Oxford.* The opening scene of the movie – in which Nick Di Angelo (Lowe) is seduced by an Older Woman, is bankrolled by her at a Las Vegas casino and given the keys to her jaunty red sports model – seems designed to reverse the impression left by *Class;* that Lowe was as irresistible to the ladies as doe-eyed fellow Brat Packer Andrew McCarthy.

The money comes in handy, because Di Angelo plans to stalk English blue-blood Lady Victoria (Amanda Pays) in the city of her education and pays a computer nerd a load of money to falsify the waiting list. This was the era, if you recall, when Americans began to fall for Olde Englishe culture in a big way. *Oxford Blues,* on one level, was the jumping-off point for a million student backpackers to flood across the Atlantic. (The other great American-backpacker-in-Britain movie was, of course, *American Werewolf in London,* from 1981.)

Ally Sheedy – fresh from *WarGames* and appearing down the bill in the Sean Penn vehicle *Bad Boys* – is the other Yank at Oxford. After getting his car wedged in an inconvenient arch, Di Angelo takes an immediate dislike to her back-talking American ways ("I didn't travel 5000 miles to spend my first morning talking to some wiseass chick from Weehawken, New Jersey.") The pugnacious Italian–American hero (this was the era of Rocky, remember) is also a rowing champ and sidles his way into Lady Victoria's affections by winning a boat race – wearing a leather jacket and perfectly knotted neck-tie! Julian Sands, before he burned his way into cinematic immortality as Helena Bonham Carter's corset invader in *Room with a View,* is on hand as Di Angelo's snotty aristocratic rival, both on the river and for Lady V's hand.

Oxford Blues is an unarguably ridiculous movie. It presents the English as a brigade of oddballs whose lives are governed by rules unfathomable by straightforward Americans. Rob Lowe never once breaks into a sweat or even ruffles his hair – despite being beaten up with a cricket bat, collapsing drunkenly in a shower and regularly performing the most energy-sapping sport known to man. But it takes the cake for its loud-hailer moralising – a world away from the emotional free-for-all of John Hughes's films. Rona (Sheedy) actually

grabs Nick and shouts into his face from a few inches away: "Can't you for once do something for someone besides yourself? It's time to grow up!" We get it.

Oxford Blues resides in the more workmanlike end of the Brat Pack spectrum; writer–director Robert Boris has enjoyed virtual anonymity ever since. Film-makers from the other set of Brats, the Movie Brats, rarely broke bread with the Brat Pack. Coppola was one exception – another was John Milius, the fire-and-sword scriptwriter–director who pulled together a cast comparable to that of *The Outsiders* for his man's-gotta-do teen thriller *Red Dawn*.

Going underground . . . Patrick Swayze, C Thomas Howell and Charlie Sheen in *Red Dawn*.

The enemy within . . . Russian
invaders in *Red Dawn*.

Most Brat Pack movies frequently allowed room for a minor rumble or two, even if great care was taken never to mark the face. Nothing symbolised a turbulent adolescence more than taking the odd battering. But *Red Dawn* took the conceit further: these kids face out their bullies with rocket-propelled grenades. Milius had just completed *Conan the Barbarian* and won plaudits earlier for the long-gestating script of *Apocalypse Now*. *Red Dawn* starts with menacing storm clouds blowing across the screen and the legend 'A Valkyrie Film'. We know where this one's headed.

C Thomas Howell and Charlie Sheen are the key faces here; they're two among a posse of school-kids who take to the hills when, in Milius' imaginative scenario, Commies start dropping from the sky in the middle of a history lesson. Giving an opening-shot nod to a statue of Theodore Roosevelt ("Far better it is to dare mighty things than to take rank among those poor timid spirits…"), *Red Dawn* is a hillbilly-militia, paranoid wet dream made flesh. While honest citizens are taken to savage "re-education camps" ("Avenge me!", screams oldster Tom Eckhert played by Harry Dean Stanton), America's brightest and best are learning the arts of survival in the back of beyond.

Much has been made of *Red Dawn*'s portrayal of its near-psychotic Commie-bashing heroes as being a tad more complex than patriotic ass-kickers of the Rambo variety – like the celebrated sequence where Jed (Patrick Swayze, replaying his tough-loving older brother character from *The Outsiders*) bloods his youthful charge Robert (Howell). In retrospect, however, *Red Dawn* is most interesting for its plausible portrayal of the chaos that would descend on any small-town American community should it ever suffer the kind of treatment US bombers have since regularly dished out in theatres of war across the globe.

Red Dawn's status as a Brat Pack movie is also somewhat tenuous. In their film work, if nothing else, both Sheen and Howell are second-division Brat Packers. Sheen's best roles in the 80s were both for Oliver Stone, in thoroughly non-Brat movies, and Howell was headed for the idiocy of *Soul Man*, and his last really good lead role, in *The Hitcher*, which was well outside the Brats' compass.

At this point too, it is necessary to bring up Ralph Macchio, another *Outsiders* alumnus. He was losing his Brat Pack status around this time; not through lack of success, but rather (like Cruise) through too much. Macchio's big shot was *The Karate Kid*, which took $90m at the box-office and resulted in his spending the rest of the decade in *Karate Kid* sequels. He became as a result too valuable a commodity to stick in the ensemble movies that were the Brat Pack's basic currency.

The Karate Kid was directed by John G Avildsen, a man whose affinity with short violent Italian–Americans had resulted, eight years earlier, in his masterminding of *Rocky* to box-office domination in 1976. Swapping the ring for the dojo, and the bloodied pug for the bullied high-schooler, Avildsen made *The Karate Kid* into a teen fable primal in its appeal. A kid reluctantly moves west, chasing the American Dream; meets a cute girl (Elisabeth Shue); gets worked over by her shit-kicking ex-boyfriend and spooky henchmen; learns to be a man; puts one over on him at the big fight. In retrospect, the depiction of the martial-arts action is rudimentary, compared to the authentic dynamism of the Chinese originals. But you can still feel the bruises when Danny Larusso (Macchio) adopts the crane stance at the climactic moment, then plants his foot in his opponent's face.

It's strange to think, in retrospect, that if Alex Cox's *Repo Man* had managed the same commercial success as *The Karate Kid*, Emilio Estevez might have exited the Brat Pack in the same way as Macchio. Estevez was making a career out of Susie Hinton adaptations – before *The Outsiders*, he had a role in 1982's *Tex* and would script and star in *That Was Then... This Is Now* – but Cox's first movie was also Estevez's first lead role of substance. *Repo Man* employed all the tropes that linked teen movies in the 80s – dysfunctional parents, tormented youth, drugs and fist-fights – but by setting it in

King of the road . . . Director Alex Cox on the set of *Repo Man*.

Speed freaks . . . Emilio Estevez and Harry Dean Stanton in *Repo Man*.

a surf punk milieu and giving it a *Kiss Me Deadly*-ish nuclear bomb plot strand, Cox put clear water between his movie and the Brat Pack genre proper.

But Estevez gave arguably his best ever performance as pissed-off punk Otto, who teams up with car repossessor Bud (perennial teen movie father-figure Harry Dean Stanton) and discovers a scumbag reality to outdo the lame posturings of his mohawked thrill-crim pals. Hoarsely intoning the phrase "In-tense!" whenever possible, Otto's antisocial odyssey has him turn his back on his family, his repo buddies and even his girlfriend Leila (Olivia Barash). *Repo Man*, however, was only a detour for Estevez who, the next year, would cement his status as a key Brat Packer in the two most crucial movies of the era.

1985

"We think you're crazy making us write an essay
telling you who we think we are. What do *you* care?"
The Breakfast Club

985 was the big one. Two era-defining films were released within months of each
other: the first in February, the second in July. Both were ensemble movies with
near-identical casts; both dealt with the troubled lives of post-adolescents making
their way through the confusing mid-1980s. Both, in their different ways, summed up the
divergent paths teen-orientated cinema was taking during this epic decade. These movies
were *The Breakfast Club* and *St Elmo's Fire*.

Finally, it seemed, these mutterings of a Hollywood gang of self-obsessed juvenile over-
achievers were borne out on screen. The Brat Pack, until now, had existed only as a loose
bunch of high-profile pals and work mates, associated by coincident appearances in
celebrity gossip columns and arrest reports. In the wider world, however, in the minds of
the poor saps who paid their money at the ticket booth, the principal casts of these two
movies were fused as one, and the Brat Pack was born.

If *St Elmo's Fire* is the arrogant, over-good-looking bastard that everyone feels good
hating, then *The Breakfast Club* is the sensitive chisel-jawed hunk with hurtin' eyes. As
already noted, John Hughes had written the script before *Sixteen Candles*, and on the
evolutionary scale, its single location and five strong characters gives it a shot-on-the-cheap
improv-workshop feel. That it's remained so long in the affection of its original audience is
testament to the success with which Hughes's arch, zinger-laced dialogue and strip-mining
of teen emotional terrain rose above its threadbare origins.

Hughes stakes out his territory from the off, with Simple Minds' Jim Kerr bellowing
Don't You Forget About Me, and a quoted lyric from David Bowie's *Changes*, "…And these
children / that you spit on / as they try to change their worlds / are immune to your
consultations, / They're quite aware / of what they're going through…" Not only is
Hughes keying into the mid-80s American high-schooler's love for posturing British pop
music, he's also encapsulating the movie's central theme. We're not dummies, old-timers,
so stop treating us like them. We can run our own lives.

In voiceover, Brian — the brain — begins to explain the assignment that brings the
Breakfast Club together. "We think you're crazy making us write an essay," he announces,
as near-documentary shots of school in progress initiate the film's visuals. In a slight
variation on the film's immortal poster line, he sets out the high-school stereotypes that
will be laid out before us: "A brain, an athlete, a basket case, a princess and a criminal."

The first sight of these five principal characters comes as they arrive, one by one, at the
start of the day's detention, and in doing so, reveal all we need to know about their

relationship with their parents – a topic that will become the most fruitful subject for their conversations as the day wears on. The princess, Claire (Molly Ringwald), whines at her dad, "I can't believe you can't get me out of this." "I'll make it up to you", he replies. "Honey, ditching class to go shopping doesn't make you a defective." The brain, Brian (Anthony Michael Hall) has a mother demanding he make the grades: "Get in there and use the time to your advantage." Andrew the athlete (Emilio Estevez) is chewed out by his father for jeopardising his chance of an college career – "No school's gonna give a scholarship to a discipline case." Basket case Allison (Ally Sheedy) is dumped, wordlessly, on the school steps. John Bender (Judd Nelson), a criminal, is on foot, and on his own.

Cue more heavy characterisation when the five assemble in the school library. Square kid Claire is sitting up front. Shy nerd Brian grabs a seat at the back. Andrew, Claire's social equal, takes the chair next to her. Bender, like the rebel he is, not only sits at the back, but forces Brian out of his chair and takes it over. Weirdo Allison sidles round three sides of a square before sitting as far in the corner as possible.

Then the talking begins. Anyone who moans that cinema in the 80s amounted to the death of dialogue and the triumph of the action jackson, should take a look at this movie. It's *all* talk. It's practically a play.

After giving them their assignment and handing out an extra Saturday's detention to Bender (for "Does Barry Manilow know you raid his wardrobe?"), teacher Richard Vernon (Paul Gleason) retires to his office behind an open door. Vernon is a summation of all that's foul and uncaring in adulthood – he's a bully, he's corrupt, and worst of all, he treats them like children. "Don't mess with the bull, young man," he sneers at Bender. "You'll get the horns."

Five strangers are left alone. Being detention kids, forced to give up a Saturday, the last thing on their minds (except for the timorous Brian) is doing any work. The ice is broken by black-clad nutball Allison munching on her fingernails; thereafter, Bender holds the floor with one disruptive act after another. His first priority, it seems, is to provoke fights – on principle – with the squares, bringing into the open the hierarchical sexual chemistry

Food fight . . . Molly Ringwald, Judd Nelson and Emilio Estevez in *The Breakfast Club*.

that Hughes has already hinted at: the sporto and the prom queen. "Do you slip her the hot… beef… injection?" he asks. It wouldn't be giving too much away to note that, since we know Bender and Claire pair off, as do Andrew and Allison, that Hughes is smart enough to put the audience on a false scent. Bender's hostility to Claire, and Andrew's protectiveness towards her, appears further indication that the latter two, natural allies, will end up together. But that's not accounting for the age-old allure of the bad boy – Bender's incessant innuendoes and salacious comments take their toll on Claire's ice-queen exterior.

It takes 33 minutes for the big question to be popped; an issue as central to 1980s teenhood as fighting with the folks. "Are you a virgin?" Bender asks Claire. "I'll bet you a million dollars that you are!" Her outrage leads directly to a major bust-up between Bender

and Andrew, with the former pulling a switchblade. Nasty.

As the movie unspools, its riches flow almost too thick and fast to count — and almost all the great lines belong to Bender. The scene where he calls Brian "a Neo-Maxi-Zoom-Dweebie". The scene where he tells Claire: "I could see you really pushing maximum density!... You see, you're gonna get married, you're gonna squeeze out a few puppies and then..." The time he asks the teacher for lunchtime refreshment: "Uh, Dick? Excuse me, Rich...will milk be made available to us?" The scene where he asks Claire if she wants to "see a picture of a guy with elephantitus of the nuts? It's pretty tasty." The spotlight is wrenched away from him only when Brian, tormented beyond endurance, confesses his own virginity.

(Opposite and above) Five alive . . *The Breakfast Club* cast.

Dope fiends . . . Molly Ringwald, Anthony Michael Hall and Judd Nelson in *The Breakfast Club*.

Things heat up. Bender acts out his violent home life. He leads them out of the library to get his stash from his locker. And, with the whole group in danger of being caught, he reveals his inner beauty, by drawing the vengeful Vernon's wrath on himself alone. What a guy.

But what brings these kids together is another eternal allure: the sweet smell of soft drugs. Bender's doobage loosens their last scruples, and some serious bonding can begin. Bender and Claire start to get cute by rummaging through each other's personal effects. Allison and Andrew mine their own previously undeclared parental difficulties ("They ignore me…" they both grizzle).

As the movie reaches its climax, Claire is taunted into revealing *her* virginity; in the longest single speech of the entire film, Andrew, deeply emotional, recounts the bullying incident that landed him in trouble ("All I could think about was Larry's father. And Larry having to go home and… and explain what happened to him"); Claire applies her lipstick from her cleavage; Bender savagely describes Christmas in his household. All of which leads up to the key utterance of the movie. "My God," asks Andrew, "are we gonna be like our parents?" "When you grow up," replies Allison, "your heart dies." Cue row upon row of teens in cinema audiences howling in recognition. There's still time for a last blazing row between Claire and Bender ("Don't you ever talk about my friends! You don't know any of my friends, you don't look at any of my friends and you certainly wouldn't condescend to speak to any of my friends!") before the movie comes roaring into its final straight.

And considering the 80 minutes of dead-eye brilliance that's come before, the i-dotting and t-crossing endgame of *The Breakfast Club* is one of the greatest letdowns in motion picture history. Not only do the entire cast launch into an idiotic freakout, but then Claire treats Allison to an appalling makeover to brush her up to Andrew's jock standards. I think I speak for an entire generation in saying that Hughes boobed big-time — apart from negating the entire each-to-their-own message of the movie, it's an indisputable fact that Ally Sheedy looked much better in her fetching, all-black get-up. In Hughes' defence, he seems to be saying that love is worth a sacrifice; a similar transformation from punkette to straight also occurs in *Pretty in Pink*, when spiky-haired record-shop worker Annie Potts dons a snow-white jacket-and-skirt ensemble to court her putative husband.

So ends one half of the Brat Pack's definitive work; an earnest, heart-wrenching depiction of fragile egos in tumult. None of these words — with the exception of egos — applies to *St Elmo's Fire*, the flip side of the Brat Pack coin. Where *The Breakfast Club* is sensitive, *St Elmo's Fire* is boorish. Where *The Breakfast Club* is restrained, *St Elmo's Fire* is over the top. Where *The Breakfast Club* is dignified, *St Elmo's Fire* is ridiculous. So it certainly seemed at the time, for *St Elmo*'s most enduring images are Rob Lowe honking idiotically on his sax, clad in a yellow vest covered in bat prints, and Demi Moore hunched catatonically in an empty room with white curtains billowing around her. And that's the accepted wisdom that's passed down the ensuing decade and a half.

In retrospect, *St Elmo's Fire* is really something. What grabs you straightaway is the unfettered looseness of all the actors involved — even Lowe, the most tight-assed of the Brat Pack. Could a clutch of today's television-schooled teen actors give the impression of being so *relaxed* in front of the camera, slip so effortlessly into their roles? Judd Nelson, Ally Sheedy and Emilio Estevez are the three transfers from *The Breakfast Club* and, while their performances naturally carry some similar elements, their characters couldn't be more different.

Apart from anything else, they're playing people at least five years older: college graduates in their early 20s, living in Washington DC, rather than neurotic high-schoolers in a Chicago suburb. Nelson is Alec Newberry, a student radical hotshot who's taken to wearing suits and sucking up to Republicans as he sets out to make his way in political circles. Sheedy is his long-time girlfriend Leslie Hunter, her *Breakfast Club* goth hairdo dyed blonde, but pulling back from being the politico's trophy wife that Alec wants. Estevez's Kirby Kager has chosen bartending as his immediate postgraduate occupation; he spends the movie in increasingly hysterical pursuit of old flame Dale Biberman (Andie MacDowell, an actress far too obviously *nice* ever to come seriously within the Brat Pack compass).

Their four compadres are as follows. Rob Lowe is Billy Hixx, a boozin', cussin', whorin' character who can't hold down a job or settle on a single girl. Mare Winningham is Wendy Beamish, the one member of the group who's turned against the whole greed-is-good thing, and who combines a do-gooder's job in a welfare office with an uncomplaining adoration (and bailing out) of Billy. Andrew McCarthy is Kevin Dolenz, a junior Hunter S Thompson figure, a wannabe wacked-out journalist who's nursing a

Gang of four . . . Andrew McCarthy, Emilio Estevez, Judd Nelson and Rob Lowe in *St Elmo's Fire*.

desire to pen an article called 'The Meaning of Life'. Lastly, Demi Moore is Jules, a good-time girl with a habit of neuroticising over her own powers of attraction *and* a wall-size poster of Billy Idol in her apartment.

Their director is Joel Schumacher, one-time costume designer (Woody Allen's *Sleeper*) and future inheritor of the *Batman* franchise (which he graced with his special high-camp body fetishism). *St Elmo's Fire* wasn't his first directorial effort, and in the great Brat Pack divide – Coppola versus Hughes – Schumacher came down decisively on the former's side. Although he was definitely in the tyro bracket, Schumacher instinctively let the camera adore his stars, showing off every pertly flexed bicep, every gently quivering nostril, every breeze-fluffed hair strand.

St Elmo's Fire opens on the magnificent seven's day of graduation from Georgetown University – school's out, life can begin. For Billy it begins with a car crash; he's taken to hospital, the gang then get together at St Elmo's Bar, the location of, and symbol for, their studenty good times. It is here the complex web of relationships within the group are first excavated. "It was a metaphysical precision collision," exults the idiotic Billy. "This thing with Billy is way too destructive," Jules tells the hopelessly fixated Wendy. "It ain't easy being me," moans the embittered Kevin. Meanwhile Kirby, the most detached of the group, embarks on the movie's narrative light-relief by running into Dr Biberman in the emergency room.

From here on in, *St Elmo's Fire* wends its way through the strings of interconnected narratives, connecting them with the kind of artful casualness that is largely lost to ensemble movies in the 90s. *St Elmo's Fire*'s individual storylines are hardly momentous drama – indeed, in many ways they're ridiculously trivial – but they're sketched in with a louche deftness and a remarkable naturalism that the Brats subsequent reputations have tended to obscure.

Kevin, for example, is widely assumed to be gay – because he hasn't got a girlfriend and spends his time mooning around Alec and Leslie's place. Jules asks him: "How come you've never made a pass at me?", then swiftly concludes: "You're gay and you're in love with Alec." She wheels in her gay neighbour to get

39

WE THINK YOU'RE CRAZY

Blow, brother, blow . . . Rob Lowe in *St Elmo's Fire*.

(Overleaf) Where the heart is . . . Andrew McCarthy and Demi Moore in *St Elmo's Fire*.

acquainted with a disbelieving Kevin. Farce turns to bitterness in the next scene when Kevin fulminates against marriage: "The notion of two people spending their entire lives together was invented by people who were lucky if they lived to 20 without being eaten by dinosaurs." Another scene sees him confront a prostitute. "How comes you don't ask me if I want a date?" "Cos I thought you were gay." We know where this is going. Turns out Kevin's carried a torch for Leslie – and, incredibly, gets what he wants when she and Alec break up. But this is the mid-1980s and not everyone can *really* get what they want; Leslie swiftly dumps him and strikes out on her own.

The rest of the movie is similarly riddled with ambitions both gratified and thwarted in the most elaborate of ways. It isn't simply, for example, that Alec destroys his relationship with Leslie by sleeping around: it's that his machiavellian, seemingly inhuman attitude to commitment can't sweep anyone else with it. Hence the extraordinary break-up scene that is alternately hilarious ("You can't have the Pretenders' first album! No Springsteen is leaving this house!") and intensely stricken. "You fucked many," Leslie accuses Alec. "Nameless, faceless many," he replies, angry.

A similar win–loss code envelops the other characters, where contentment achieved is inversely proportional to the assurance with which they face the future. Champion in this regard is Jules, the self-dramatising party chick, who early on provides a crisp summary of where she's headed, after being cautioned against sleeping with her boss. "This is the 80s. Bop him for a few years; get his job when he gets caught with his hand in the vault; become a legend; do a Black Mink ad; write a huge best-seller and become a fabulous host of my own talk show." By the end of the movie, it's revealed she's an out-and-out faker: no job, no money, no life. "I never thought I'd be so tired at 22," she moans piteously. "I just don't know who to be anymore."

Appropriately enough, at this climatic juncture, it's only honking hepcat Billy who can provide her with any comfort. Quickly pegged as never-grow-up funster ("Four months after graduation, and you're still acting like every night's a frat party"), he soon recognises that cracks in the facade are beginning to appear. "School was pretty out of hand," he complains, "in everyday life there's just no way to be out of hand." After fucking up one time too many, he goes back to the sports fields of his youth looking for validation. In a downbeat payoff, "Billy the kid" is told they need him – to get them drugs.

It's also Billy who provides the ambiguous moral coda to the movie, as enshrined in the title. Cradling the fucked-up Jules, he tells her: "This isn't real: it's St Elmo's Fire… They made it up to keep themselves going when things get tough." In other words, he says, wilful self-deception is the only way. And nothing is more 1980s than that. The 1980s may have been the decade of greed, ambition, and self-obsession; but it was also the decade of built-in irony. Reaching for that long-cherished desire, that eternally nurtured dream, also means discovering the bitter pill contained therein: and everyone knew it.

* * * * *

And geek created woman . . .
Anthony Michael Hall, Kelly
LeBrock and Ilan Mitchell-Smith in
Wierd Science.

Weird Science became a television series during the teen-movie renaissance of the mid-1990s, but it was also the second film John Hughes released in 1985. Although it features prime Brat Packer Anthony Michael Hall seemingly only a few months after his *Breakfast Club* immortality, as well as putative Packer Robert Downey Jr sneering his way into public consciousness as a high-school bully-boy, there's something about the movie that shuts it out from the Brat Pack roll of honour.

Partly it's down to the fact that, after completing *Breakfast Club*, Hall's growth hormones appeared to kick in with disconcerting speed – so that the fresh-faced geekoid charm he displayed in both that movie and *Sixteen Candles* starts to disappear before our very eyes. In *Weird Science* he's a sunken-cheeked string-bean with hair that badly needs washing – by the time of *Edward Scissorhands*, a mere five years later, he's an unrecognisable slab of beef. Moreover, *Weird Science* doesn't even pretend to be a howl of teen angst – it's just another one of those movies about Losin' It, albeit with a higher-than-usual proportion of well-carved zingers.

Gary (Hall) and Wyatt (Ilan Mitchell-Smith) are the high-school virgins, routinely mocked and humiliated, who plug a Barbie doll into a computer and – one lightning strike later – are in possession of Lisa (Kelly LeBrock), a hot-to-trot sorceress with a mission to find the guys both girlfriends *and* street credibility. Hughes ploughs through one self-consciously zany set piece after another, but little if anything catches fire – skewered by the charmlessness of the leads and LeBrock's inability to time a comic line. In a climactic party scene, Gary and Wyatt see off a posse of demented bikers, snare a couple of babes for themselves and end up with a nuclear missile speared through the house. It sounds funnier in summary than it actually is.

1986

"I'm so humiliated; I walked right into it."

About Last Night

In 1986 it became clear that the Brat Pack had lost its innocence. After the heady heights of 1985 and its double-masterwork triumph, the Brat Pack had become a label. Nothing destroys a label faster than it becoming a journalist's plaything. As 1986 dawned, the Brat Pack were already rebelling against it, denying there ever was a Brat Pack and showing considerable reluctance ever to get involved with their fellow Brat Packers again. Fortunately for civilisation, however, there were movies already in the can.

Step forward John Hughes. As already mentioned, Hughes had written the script for *Pretty in Pink* as *The Breakfast Club* was being readied for release, with the twin inspirations of Molly Ringwald's preferred wardrobe palette and one of her favourite tunes, by The Psychedelic Furs. In the event, Hughes handed the directorial reins to music video maker Howard Deutch. Hughes was snowed under with directing work, gearing up to shoot *Ferris Bueller's Day Off* early in the year.

Pretty in Pink made it into theatres in February 1986. Although using the same basic template as *Sixteen Candles* – a high-school girl yearns longingly for older boy – Hughes nudged the script towards a more considered, mature approach to the travails of true love. For one thing, Ringwald herself looked much older than *Sixteen Candles'* 16-year-old who'd collapsed into an emotional maelstrom when her family forgot her birthday. She also looked tougher, more self-possessed. Moreover, whereas peer-group pressure and family history held the stage in *The Breakfast Club*, in *Pretty in Pink*, Hughes gropes towards all-out socio-economic analysis.

Ringwald plays Andie, a girl who lives (literally) on the wrong side of the tracks, with her washed-up, unemployed pop (perennial teen-movie father figure Harry Dean Stanton, taking the money and running). Mom is nowhere around, having decamped years earlier. Taking on the Anthony Michael Hall role is Jon Cryer; he plays Duckie, Andie's geek-motormouth friend – himself desperately, yearningly in love with her.

It swiftly becomes apparent that there's a fiscal divide among the high-school students. Andie, Duckie and the rest of the stoners, punks and poetry-readers, versus the upscale, high-tone suits and squares. It's across this divide that Andie's eyes lock with a set of baby blues belonging to Blane (Andrew McCarthy), when he wanders into the record shop where she works. "Would you ever consider going out with someone who had money?" she wonders out loud later, before setting out for a drive with Duckie to drool over the town's fanciest properties ("I bet the people who live there don't think it's as pretty as I do.") Hence the emotional battle-lines are drawn:

The Duckman cometh . . . Jon Cryer in *Pretty in Pink*.

Andie hates herself for admitting the allure of the green stuff, but Blane is *so cute*…

Blane and Andie eventually organise a date. When he finds out, Duckie is naturally distraught. (His scene, wailing, "I love this woman and I have to tell her…" is one of the most painful thwarted-emotion moments in teen-movie history.) Equally appalled is Blane's pal Stef (James Spader), a sneering rich kid already rejected by Andie. "My best friend, conversing with a mutant?" he observes. Echoing the words of *Sixteen Candles*' Jake, Blane replies: "You don't think she's got something?" – thereby enshrining Ringwald as the epitome of elusive junior allure. What was this "something" that high-school seniors got so worked up about? The red hair? The bee sting mouth? The stream of cuss-words that readily exploded from it? Who knows – all that mattered is that John Hughes thought he was onto something, and in three successive movies made Molly Ringwald the casing for his essays in easily mortified, dignity-obsessed, high-school dream queen. And we are all the richer.

Pretty in Pink, however, remains Hughes' most concrete statement on class war in the classroom. Andie explains to the school head teacher the reason behind the friction in her tutorial group: "I don't like my friends getting dumped on or punished for defending themselves." "Andie," he replies, "if you put out signals that you don't want to belong, people will make sure you don't." "That's a beautiful theory," she snaps back. Here we see developed an analysis hinted at in *The Breakfast Club*, that school tribalism is as fragmented and Darwinian as in society outside, and that institutions are not the unifying force they seem to be. Although *Pretty in Pink*, like practically every other US movie of its ilk, is neurotically obsessed by its central characters' attendance or otherwise at the end-of-year prom, it's one of the rare movies to suggest that it *serves* a particular social grouping – a sort of works' outing for the conventionally minded – rather than a compulsory test that everyone has to pass.

Hence *Pretty in Pink*'s unpitying inspection of another perennial teen-movie staple: friends. Angst over popularity is *the* connecting thread of the genre – successful kids have it, nerds want and need it. In *The Breakfast Club*, the detainees' row over whether their bond will survive through to normal school life ("Be honest, Andy," says Claire, "If Brian came walking up to you in the hall on Monday, what would you do?"). In *Pretty in Pink*, Andie and Blane's attachment has to surmount the hostility of both sets of friends. Duckie is openly contemptuous, as well as heart-broken ("His name is Blane? That's a major appliance, not a name.") The pair's first date turns into an ordeal of tribal disapproval – "I can't believe I associate with these people," says Blane, after Andie is frozen out at the upscale party they attend. "I overestimated my friends." Blane fares equally badly when Andie drags him along to her regular haunt, one of those weird punk clubs that exist only in teen movies. The night culminates in Andie's heart-wrenching outburst – "I don't want to you to see where I live, okay!" – as her insecurities about the "richies" overcome her.

Here the movie takes a twist: the weak-willed Blane, with Stef pouring venom in his ear, backs off. In Hughes' eyes, clearly, he embodies the equivocal virtues of the well-off: access to the finer things in life but, as Andie has pointed out about their housing, unable to appreciate them. When she finally corners him, her strength of character and emotional integrity is made clear. "You're a liar," she yells. "You're a filthy fucking no-good liar!" (One of Ringwald's many talents is to spew obscenities as naturally as a real-life teen – Brat Pack movies don't filter out the cuss-words at all.)

It's all nicely set up for the much mulled-over ending, which was tested and replaced before release. Andie shows up at the prom in her home-made dress, Duckie on her arm – "I just want to let them know they didn't break me." Originally, *Pretty in Pink* ended here, with the accent on Andie's psychological victory over her tormentors. Naturally, however, audiences wanted to see Andie and Blane get together, and although the ending that Hughes eventually conjured up may, perhaps unfairly, redeem the rich kid, it converts *Pretty in Pink* into one of the all-time great teen fairy tales.

Like any set of unruly teens, however, the Brat Pack had to grow up. Where *St Elmo's Fire* chronicled the first faltering steps of a bunch of college grads in the big bad world, *About Last Night…* dispensed entirely with educational institutions and concentrated on working girls and stiffs to the exclusion of all else.

(Opposite) The colour of money . .
Molly Ringwald in *Pretty in Pink*.

Credited as an adaptation of David Mamet's play *Sexual Perversity in Chicago*, *About Last Night...* represents the Brat Pack's most serious attempt yet to get to grips with adulthood. It stars Rob Lowe and Demi Moore in somewhat more downbeat versions of their roles in *St Elmo's Fire*: Danny (Lowe) is a salesman who is not as motivated as he once was in the dating game; Debbie (Moore) is an advertising-agency minionwho is sleeping with her boss and is sick of it. The pair lock eyes at a softball game in the park, then hook up for real at a post-game drinking session.

Counterpointing this central pair are their same-sex pals. Danny has Bernie (James Belushi), a big lug of a guy who's forever promoting his fuck-'em-and-chuck-'em ideology; Debbie has Joan (Elizabeth Perkins), bitter and suspicious to the end. Both, naturally, can't bear to see their friends' relationship flowering and do everything in their power to bring it down.

The morning after . . . Demi Moore (opposite) and Moore and Rob Lowe (left) in *About Last Night . . . .*

To its credit, *About Last Night...* refuses the temptation to go all upscale, keeping its characters stuck in the kind of low-grade, dead-end jobs that are entirely appropriate to their unhappy world-view. There's more than a hint of the desperation of *Glengarry Glen Ross* in Danny and Bernie's polyester-shirted work room. And even though she's bopping her boss, Debbie hardly looks in line for a Black Mink advert. These are the sort of young adults who can only dream about being yuppies – "washed up at 24," Danny moans at one point; a considerable comedown from the sort of futures promised to the glowing teens the Brat Packers were playing a year or two earlier.

About Last Night... explicitly handles the transition from swinging singlehood, where these things don't matter, to commitment and settling down, where they do. "The best thing that could happen to you," Bernie tells Danny, "is an industrial accident." Danny's so good-looking, it seems, that he makes girls

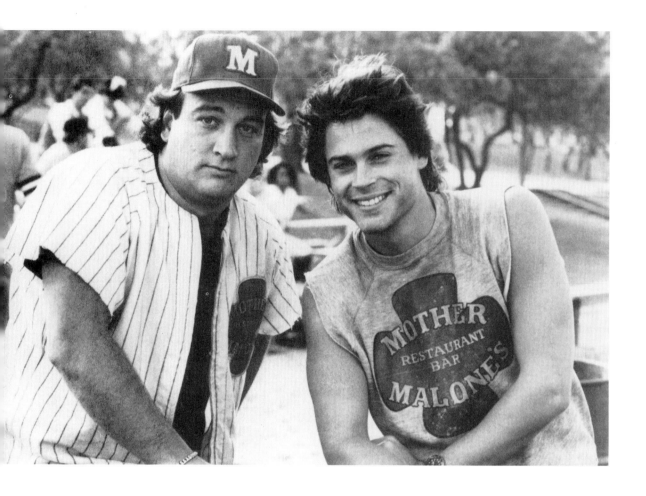

Take me out to the ballgame . . .
James Belushi and Rob Lowe in
About Last Night . . . .

nervous. "They feel dumpy. They don't want to compete." This doesn't intimidate Debbie, however, and when she and Danny finally do the dirty, the stage is set for dipping their toes in the heady waters of long-term relationship. At first it's all tricky defensiveness. "Don't look at me like the cat who ate the canary," Debbie snaps, "because this is as far as this goes tonight."

Slowly and painfully the pair come closer together, with Bernie and Joan providing a bitchy background mutter. "Men and women are fighting for their lives," counsels Joan. "The sexes relate in a very violent way." Despite the intimidation, the lovebirds go ahead with their cohabitation; surprise, surprise, the moment that responsibility and nurturing comes in the door, affection and happiness flies out the window. It's Danny's closed-off maleness that's the relationship's principal wrecking ball: Debbie wants some mutual caring-and-sharing which he can't, or won't, deliver. "It's wrong," she wails, "that I don't know you very well. I'm sneaking through your drawers looking for pieces of I don't know what."

Their relationship quickly becomes a slippery slope – sticking together means plodding on through the symbols of domesticity, which brings with it proportionate levels of misery and unhappiness. Danny gets nostalgic for his beer-swilling bachelor days – "You don't go here, you don't go there… you're about as much fun as a stick", Bernie tells him. It's the archetypal American family event, Thanksgiving, that initiates the relationship's meltdown. "I hate that number they play," Debbie rails to Joan. "I feel like a fire hydrant that's been pissed on."

From here on in, slow death awaits. They finally end it after a set of rows on New Year's Eve; it's just as ironic as Thanksgiving, since New Year's Eve is the movies' favourite time for warm feelings and cute kisses. Cue breakdown of Danny's hitherto sullen disregard for the sloppier side of life; the guy can't believe the tide of love and remorse that sweeps over him. "Everything is falling apart, because I miss you," he bleats down the phone at her. But Debbie is inflexible. "Get on with your life, it's over."

At last it seems a Brat Pack movie is giving us life tough and lived, where there are no happy endings, no hugs, no redemption. Fat chance. Danny quits his job and realises his dream of setting up a restaurant. Bernie buries the hatchet and loots a load of catering supplies to help his old buddy. And *About Last Night…* ends where it began, at a softball game in the park. Debbie and Joan cycle by, Danny looks across… "We really ripped it to shreds, didn't we?" coos Debbie, as a prelude to an unlikely reunion. And the movie closes with Danny chasing her into the distance.

Despite its weirdly out-of-kilter ending, *About Last Night…* remains one of the most convincing of the Brat Pack movies: it offers a chastened exploration of its subject, with a uniquely miserable slant on the dating game. There's none of the impassioned agony that flows through John Hughes' films; nor do its characters inhabit some enchanted world of fantastic jobs and freaky lifestyles. Even Rob Lowe's as-vapid-as-normal performance seems appropriate for a character unable to discern his own shallowness, let alone that of the milieu he inhabits.

*   *   *   *   *

No such ironies are present in *Youngblood*, a movie Lowe squeezed in between *St Elmo's Fire* and *About Last Night…* Scratching Lowe's jock itch (presumably, films like this and *Oxford Blues* were made to counter accusations that he never got his hands dirty), *Youngblood* is that can't-fail beast – an ice-hockey movie. Ice hockey's got it all: speed, violence, conflict and washed-up sportos by the fistful.

Although it's no *Slap Shot*, *Youngblood* is considerably superior to most Brat-Packer-going-it-alone products. Lowe plays the eponymous aspirant hockey ace, first name Dean, who tries out for a Canadian junior league team. His dead eye for goal gets him a place in the squad; his designs on the coach's daughter Jessica (Cynthia Gibb) ensure he spends most of the season cooling his heels on the bench. (His and Jessica's first encounter is one of the all-time classic Meet Cutes: he's locked out of the changing room clad only in an athletic support and a small towel. The towel falls off.) Among Youngblood's fellow skate pack are Patrick Swayze, doing another older-brother-to-the-Brats role, and a callow

Ice ice baby . . . Rob Lowe and Cynthia Gibb in *Youngblood*.

Keanu Reeves. You don't need to see the movie to know that *Youngblood* overcomes all obstacles to inspire his team to win the Big Game – "Rocky on ice" was the general critical reaction at the time – but *Youngblood* isn't as all-round idiotic as *Oxford Blues*.

What were the other Brats doing in 1986? Emilio Estevez took a lead role in Stephen King's directorial debut, *Maximum Overdrive*, in which machines turn on humanity after an asteroid impact. In the trailers, King notoriously bragged "I'm going to scare the hell out of you," but only succeeded in metaphorically hanging Estevez out to dry in a tension-free cliché magnet. It took a proper director, Rob Reiner, to show how to really adapt a King story in the entirely Brat-free *Stand By Me*, also released this year. Judd Nelson, meanwhile, made the first of a string of doomed attempts to re-ignite his *Breakfast Club/St Elmo's* firecracker performances in *Blue City*. He plays a dislikeable mayor's son out to track down his dad's killers. Ally Sheedy, caged once again in a support role considerably beneath her, is a cute cop who helps him. Her Brat Pack career never recovered.

It is only tangential to the Brat Pack canon proper, but *Ferris Bueller's Day Off* deserves inspection as a modulation in John Hughes' thinking and an important

3- 5029-6

entry in the 80s teen cycle. Released in June 1986, it has Matthew Broderick – never a paid-up Brat Packer – as the incorrigibly charming teen of the title. No hint of parent-hating rebellion sullies his dementedly perfect personality ("Sportos, metalheads, geeks, sluts, buds, dweebies, wastoids, they all adore him," explains a school administrator); his ma and pa, it would seem, are just pawns in Ferris' game in taking some time off school. All Hughes' emotional constipation is the prerogative of Ferris' pal Cameron, whose Ferrari-owning dad is a never-seen monster of trauma-inspiration.

Broderick puts in the performance of a lifetime – and so, thankfully, do a supporting cast that includes Jeffrey Jones as school head Ed Rooney ("I did not achieve this position in life by having some snot-nosed punk leave my cheese out in the wind"), Jennifer Grey as a classic Hughesian resentful sibling, and (what's this?) Charlie Sheen in a tiny role as a junkie loafing around a police station. Having got this zinger-spouting apotheosis of sunny ebullience out of his system, Hughes had one more teen-misery movie left in him. That would have to wait until the next year.

Master and pupil . . .
John Hughes and Matthew
Broderick on the set of *Ferris
Bueller's Day Off.*

1987

"You did it to yourself, and you know it."

Less Than Zero

As 1987 dawned, it was clear that the Brat Pack movies had reached some sort of crossroads. The actors themselves were getting older and finding it harder to impersonate angry young grads permanently on the brink of entering the real world. The Brat Pack tag was onerous, too: the fresh-faced callowness that served them so well only months earlier was being submerged under a tide of hormones, worry lines and fancy new haircuts. Taste, they knew, was liable to change at any minute – if they didn't keep moving, they could get caught with their pants down. And not just on videotape.

Little did they know it, but many of the original Brat Pack had already reached their peak, had already done all they were going to do. The next year or two would see their increasingly flailing attempts to ride the monster wave they'd created, largely without success. Previously marginal figures – in cinematic terms at least – would move to centre stage, satisfying the movies' eternal demands for new flesh for the meat grinder.

This, clearly, is what lies behind the symbolic passing of the Brat Pack baton that occurs in *Less Than Zero*. Strange as it may seem, of all the *Breakfast Club / St Elmo's Fire* group, only Andrew McCarthy was singled out by fate to see the light of day ever again in a half-decent Brat Pack movie. And nestling up next to him were the puppy-dog eyes of Robert Downey Jr, an actor who would take the Brat Pack to new heights.

Less Than Zero was adapted from Bret Easton Ellis' debut novel, an eerie, haunting book that managed to gouge a mysterious sense of regret from the activities of a bunch of wastoid rich kids denatured by affluence. While no one would ever claim that the movie approaches the original in anatomising the soulless emotional landscape of the mid-80s, it's got a lot going for it.

The threat to adolescent relationships – of all kinds – posed by the inevitable relocation to a college campus is the unspoken menace hanging over many a teen movie. Remember Ferris Bueller's prognostication about his and Cameron's future? ("We're going to graduate in a couple of months, and then we'll have the summer. He'll work and I'll work, we'll see each other at night and at the weekends. Then he'll go to one school and I'll go to another. Basically, that'll be it.") *Less Than Zero*, in movie form, approaches this territory directly, using the dislocation of college study to kickstart a story about a post-teen love triangle whose principals take a major step down the road to dead-hearted adult loss of innocence.

Like *St Elmo's Fire*, *Less Than Zero* opens with a graduation ceremony, but at a high-school Class of '87 rather than Georgetown University. Julian (Downey), Clay and Clay's girl Blair (Jami Gertz) are among the graduands who interrupt their principal's address with shouts of "We want money!" Flash forward six months: Clay is preparing to go to LA for Christmas from his East Coast college, haunted by memories of Blair and Julian's betrayal ("How much time did it take you to fuck my best friend?") Nevertheless, Clay's is a heart that does not die, and he heads back West to try to connect once again with his former girlfriend.

There he's greeted by the spectacle that held critics in 1987 enthralled and heralded Robert Downey Jr as a major star. Julian, it seems, is in trouble: he owes $50,000 to a drug dealer called Rip (James Spader, reworking his *Pretty in Pink* sneer, only with a slicked-back 'do), his dad has thrown him out the house and, worst of all, he'll lie, cheat and steal to fund his out-of-control cocaine addiction. Roger Ebert, writing in the *Chicago Sun Times*, noted that Downey's performance "is so real, so subtle and so observant that it's scary." Enough said.

Clay is drawn into Julian's personal melodrama, fending off Rip and his goons, and rescuing Julian when it's apparent that he's being forced into prostitution. Nostalgia, wistfulness and memory of the teenage good times are the key elements of their relationship, and that's what makes *Less Than Zero* such an impressively bitter tract. Julian is irredeemable, but Clay and Blair unhesitatingly commit their loyalty to him, even as they doubt his justifications. "Rip made me do it. I didn't have a choice," Julian protests, as Clay hustles him out of a boy-on-boy clinch. "Shit, man," retorts Clay, "you did it. You did it to yourself, and you know it."

Loyalty to friends, you begin to suspect, acts as a kind of moral touchstone in a milieu that's lost all sense of restraint. Blair, coke-addled and faithless, is almost pathetic in her reflex insistence that Julian needs looking after. The environment has also left its indelible mark on Julian – "Do I look like I'm ready for homework?" he lashes out in desperation when Clay suggests taking him out of LA to his college. *Less Than Zero* is one of those films that offers a seductive vision of decadence, while simultaneously critiquing it and, suitably for this most thematically ambitious of teen movies, it's one of the few of the genre that offers much in the way of cinematic style. Director Marek Kanievska, who started out on the television show *Hazell* and scored a hit with the Rupert Everett movie *Another Country* piles on the glossy visuals, presumably to suggest the hedonism without and vacuity within. Like *American Gigolo*, a not dissimilar paean to an empty-headed, empty-hearted society, *Less Than Zero* possesses an surface sheen that's totally distinctive, the kind of movie that you could instantly recognise without knowing its identity. A real original.

Two months earlier, in September, movie audiences were treated to arguably the most wretched effort of the entire Brat Pack era. Films in 1987 did their best to lower the boom on the Pack. Films like *From the Hip* (Judd Nelson as a lawyer), *Mannequin* (Andrew McCarthy as a store clerk in love with a shop dummy) and *Wisdom* (Emilio Estevez and Demi Moore as Bonnie and Clyde-esque crime celebrities). *The Pick-Up Artist*, however, is in a nauseating class of its own as a flagrant abuse of the gifts of its performers. In Molly Ringwald it had the hottest star in America – practically a national monument after making the cover of *Time* magazine. Whatever his recreational activities, Robert Downey Jr could burn up the screen if given the opportunity. Harvey Keitel and Dennis Hopper are both on hand to flesh out the supporting roles. The blame for this sorry farrago must lie with writer–director James Toback.

Toback had won raves a decade earlier with his debut feature *Fingers* (starring Keitel as an ivory-tickler caught up in the Mob), and presumably conceived *The Pick-Up Artist* as a comic paean to the legendary lechery of his mentor Warren Beatty. Indeed, it was Beatty who persuaded Ringwald to appear, dithering as she was about how to break out of the teen-princess mould that had served her so well. She plays museum guide Randy Jensen, a tough cookie who exerts an unnatural fascination for Jack Jericho (Downey) – a schoolteacher so craven for female attention that he approaches practically every woman he meets.

While the plot that develops from their encounter – Randy's father owes a mobster a lot of money and Jack helps his initially reluctant conquest to find it – is merely uninspired, where *The Pick-Up Artist* really falls apart is in its treatment of its central character. Jericho's woman-hassling ways are presented in a sort of light comedy, permanently amused vein – when, in reality, Jericho is the kind of self-absorbed predator who would permanently be on the edge of a sexual harrassment suit.

Truth to tell, *The Pick-Up Artist* killed both Ringwald and Toback's careers stone dead: Toback wouldn't direct another dramatic feature for a decade (reuniting with Downey for *Two Girls and a Guy* in 1997), while Ringwald managed to dissipate the goodwill of an entire generation with this abortive attempt to fashion an adult screen persona. (Playing Cordelia in Jean Luc Godard's *King Lear* probably didn't help either.) Superficially, *The Pick-Up Artist* ranges over the same thematic material – relationships, angst, true love, parental friction – that is central to the Brat Pack movie, but Toback's cinematic obnoxiousness converted them into a foul broth.

On the other hand, Joel Schumacher – the hair-and-make-up merchant behind *St Elmo's Fire* – proved his affinity with the Brat Pack generation by weighing in with *The Lost Boys* in the summer of 1987. Kiefer Sutherland had been noodling around the edges of Brat Pack cinema for some time without ever really busting in (the closest he got was playing the bully kid in *Stand by Me*), until Schumacher put him into Billy Idol peroxide as David, lead biker of a pack of long-haired vampires.

The Lost Boys, unlike most Brat Pack movies, doesn't have any aspirations to analysing the post-adolescent condition – unless you call moodily floating up to the ceiling in mid-nap, as newly vamped Mike (Jason Patric) does at one point, a metaphor for hormone-racked youngsters' bemusement at the changes their bodies are going through. It fits – sort of. Chief among Mike's lusts is tangle-haired vampette Star (Jami Gertz – 1987 was her year, clearly); theirs swiftly becomes one of those tormented teen relationships when it becomes apparent that neither she nor Mike will go the whole hog and bite human neck, as David

She's got it . . . Molly Ringwald in *The Pick-up Artist*.

Love like blood . . . Kiefer
Sutherland (above) and with Jami
Gertz in *The Lost Boys*
(opposite).

commands. Schumacher keeps everything characteristically luscious, with lots of
neon lighting, dry ice and flowing hair; and there's a scene set in an abandoned
hotel resort that's eerily reminiscent of the grandiose sets he would build for
Batman & Robin. If nothing else, *The Lost Boys* demonstrates that Brat Pack cinema
was falling back on genre hybrid to sustain itself – a clear sign that it was running
out of steam and surrendering itself to a kind of creative decadence. The
flash–trash end of the Brat Pack, which Schumacher's films most perfectly
symbolised, was becoming more trash than flash.

The other side of the Brat Pack coin, the heartfelt Hughesian strand, also reached
the end of the road in 1987 with *Some Kind of Wonderful*, released in February. The
same combination behind *Pretty in Pink* – words by John Hughes, direction by
Howard Deutch – conspired to produce a distillation of all that Hughes had set out
to achieve in his string of movies examining teenage life – and in doing so, rendered
the genre practically redundant.

The clearest sign that the party was over was that none of the principal cast that
made Hughes' earlier films so memorable was involved. No Nelson, no McCarthy,

no Sheedy and, most significantly, no Ringwald. Instead he cast Eric Stoltz, who'd starred in *Mask* and been dumped from the lead in *Back to the Future*. The lineage of The Geek and The Duckman was continued in the shape of Mary Stuart Masterson, playing a besotted sidekick. The necessary third arm of the triangle – the equivalent, if you will, to hunky seniors Blane and Jake – was Lea Thompson, perky gunslinger in *Red Dawn* and Lorraine Baines in *Back to the Future*. (She'd have played Stoltz's mom, had he kept the role in that movie.)

As is readily apparent, Hughes is working with the same three-way narrative structure that fuelled his *Sixteen Candles* and *Pretty in Pink*. Arguably, this is Hughes' most classical example, evolving out of the schematics of his first teen movie script, *The Breakfast Club*. Keith, "a weird guy in a huge school" is wedded to his painting; his father, a summary of all the parents of *The Breakfast Club* kids, expects him to make something of himself at business school ("You got a shot to be the first guy in this family who doesn't have to wash his hands after a day's work.")

Keith loses his heart to Amanda Jones, a high-schooler who runs with the richies – a reworking, quite clearly, of *Pretty in Pink*'s class antagonism. ("Chicks like that," Keith is told, "have one thing on their mind, and you don't make enough of it.") Peer pressure weighs heavily on them from both sides, but the pair stumble into courtship (she's quarrelled with her boorish boyfriend Hardy). But after Keith figures she's a pawn in Hardy's plan to give him a beating, his big date with her turns into a *Pretty in Pink* prom-style crusade to prove himself to the rich kids.

Running parallel to this, however, is the unrequited affection felt for Keith by his tomboyish girl buddy Watts. Although Watts is kind of ridiculous, she's thoroughly dignified compared to her predecessors Duckie and Farmer Ted, and she's not simply comic relief. Hanging in there to help Keith out on his plans to snare Amanda, she bottles her emotion – only to let it out in a truly heart-rending confrontation. "I'd rather not see you and have you think good things about me," she weeps, "than have you see me and hate me. I can't afford to have you hate me."

When the movie arrives at its climax, Hughes has arranged things so that the weaknesses of *Pretty in Pink* – that forced his hand over the ending – have been eliminated. Keith has his moral victory over the richies – humiliating Hardy and impressing Amanda – but can maintain emotional commitment to the blue-collar kids by switching his affection to the lovelorn Watts. (Amanda turns out to be not quite so well-off after all, making her relationship with Keith less starkly incongruous than Blane and Andie's in *Pretty in Pink*.) The gender reversal of the central characters appears to be the key ingredient; since Hughes is always concerned to stress the power of female desire and emotion, he makes Watts into a far more viable mate for his lead than the Duckman or the Geek.

But in its perfection of theme and plot, *Some Kind of Wonderful* sounded the death knell for the Brat Pack. John Hughes' next movie would be *Planes, Trains and Automobiles*, and with his defection, the teen movie's most outstanding supporter bowed out. By the end of 1987, the Brat Pack was left twisting in the wind. The sands were running out.

Affairs of the heart . . . Lea Thompson and Eric Stoltz in *Some Kind of Wonderful*.

And after?

To all intents and purposes, the Brat Pack ceased to exist in 1988. The actors themselves were all functioning and perfectly employable, but the key factors that engineered their rise had largely disappeared. For one, the teen movie boom itself was largely exhausted, growing old and stale like the Pack themselves. Careers also took divergent turns, meaning that the ensemble casts that sustained the likes of *The Breakfast Club* were no longer feasible. And while, Hydra-like, new performers arose to become stars in their own right off the back of teen-orientated movies, the likes of Winona Ryder, Keanu Reeves and Julia Roberts weren't about to allow themselves to be pigeonholed in the same way as their predecessors.

In 1988, Molly Ringwald made two further attempts to resuscitate her catastrophically waning star. *For Keeps* had her as a high-schooler whose promising collegiate career is suddenly thrown off track when she becomes pregnant. In *Fresh Horses* she plays a white trash mall rat who is the subject of already affianced straight arrow Andrew McCarthy. Neither worked, and Ringwald's cause was lost.

The final significant shot in the Brat Pack locker was a western, *Young Guns*, which pulled together Emilio Estevez, Charlie Sheen and Keifer Sutherland. They, along with Lou Diamond Phillips, Dermot Mulroney and Casey Siemaszko, form "The Regulars", a band of youthful gunslingers out to avenge the killing of their mentor John Tunstall (Terence Stamp). Like *The Lost Boys*, *Young Guns* was a genre piece that conclusively demonstrated the bankruptcy of Brat Pack cinema. There was nothing about it that provoked even the remotest empathy with its teen audience; it was a story that could have been told with actors of any age; and, confused plotting and incoherent narrative aside, it made its stars look ridiculously out of depth. Where Sam Peckinpah, George Roy Hill and Arthur Penn had moseyed tall, director Christopher Cain merely stumbled around the cactus patch. Though Estevez, Sheen and co – in keeping with Brat Pack tradition – played their characters like hoodlums who only needed a few sessions with a rage therapy counsellor, this tale of Billy the Kid's formative years lacks all those qualities of grit, dirt and desperation that might have made it work.

Ironically, the Brats' public profile helped *Young Guns* to a $44m box-office take, and made a sequel, *Young Guns II*, a necessity. But by 1990, when that movie saw the light of day, the Brat Pack was history. What happened? Essentially, careers that were at one point running in tandem, had diverged to the point that the unity of the Pack had disintegrated beyond repair.

Of the original crew, it was Emilio Estevez with the two *Young Guns* movies who held on to the Brat Pack tag for the longest. Mostly because, in doing films like

Stakeout (1987), *Men at Work* (1990) and *Freejack* (1992), he was developing a career
as a respectable performer in undistinguished films. In 1992 he found a franchise –
The Mighty Ducks – that kept him in pay cheques through the rest of the decade. The
most recent (and Estevez's most recent head-above-ramparts appearance) was *D3* in
1996 (he also appeared briefly, and uncredited, alongside his old mucker from
The Outsiders, Tom Cruise, in *Mission: Impossible*). Estevez also racked up a number of
directorial credits, including the recent *The War at Home* (1996). Most people, though,
identify Estevez the auteur with *Men at Work* (1990), the one where he and brother
Charlie play garbage collectors.

As for the one-time Carlos Estevez, his tabloid-fodder lifestyle has ironically
earned him a screen career of considerable substance. Only a bit-part player in the
Brat Pack's finer cinematic moments, Charlie Sheen came into his own with an
Oliver Stone one–two, in 1986 and 1987. He did good work for another name
director, John Sayles, in the baseball-corruption drama *Eight Men Out*, before
occasionally attempting to cross over into straight thriller territory. These never came
to much: from *Navy SEALS* (1990), through *Terminal Velocity* (1994), to *Shadow
Conspiracy* (1997), it was clear that no one could really see him as a hero. Sheen's off-
screen behaviour meant comedy was more his style, and he found his metier in the

1990s in various *Hot Shots!* and *Loaded Weapons* spoofs. He recently mastered the art of the celebrity cameo in the much-admired *Being John Malkovich* ("Truth is for suckers, Johnny Boy").

Kiefer Sutherland, the Estevezs' compadre in *Young Guns*, has had a similarly choppy subsequent career. He took a support slot in *Bright Lights, Big City* (1988), a fundamentally misconceived attempt to go over *Less Than Zero* ground (Michael J Fox as a blow-addict? Say it ain't so…), and the British-set *Chicago Joe and the Showgirl* (1990) – a flop which, if nothing else, showed that Sutherland couldn't be trusted to carry a movie. Sensibly, he's since stuck to weird-but-interesting character parts: in *Flatliners* (1990), *Twin Peaks: Fire Walk With Me* (1992) and, most recently, as a nutso doctor in *Dark City* (1998). Against the odds, the guy's got a career.

As does Rob Lowe. The wretched humiliation surrounding the circulation of the notorious videotape of Lowe in action with a female fan appeared to have abruptly terminated his screen career in the late 80s. But after a few floundering years, Lowe, like Charlie Sheen, adroitly began to trade on his trashed reputation. In *Wayne's World* (1992), he unveiled a self-satisfied, deceitful screen character that he would reprise in *Tommy Boy* (1992). Mike Myers gave him further work in both *Austin Powers* movies to date (1997, 1999), and has employed his slippery qualities to acclaim in the television series *The West Wing*, playing a White House spin doctor.

Mare Winningham, on the other hand, who played Lowe's devoted protector in *St Elmo's Fire*, had only a tangential relationship with Brat Pack cinema after 1985. Most of her pay cheques have come from television movie world (titles like *She Stood Alone*, *Betrayed by Love* and *Letter to my Killer* stand out). Winningham has occasionally surfaced in the cinema, playing support roles in *Turner and Hooch* and *Wyatt Earp*. The most notable entry on her resume, however, is the title role in *Georgia* (1995), where she played a successful singer who sparks sibling rivalry in little sister Jennifer Jason Leigh.

Television has also sustained the recent career of *St Elmo's/Breakfast Club* alumnus Judd Nelson. His work conspicuously spiralled ever lower after that heady double. After failures like *From the Hip* (1988), the only films of note he got his face in during the following decade were *New Jack City* (1991) and *Airheads* (1994). But a four-year stint (1996–99) on Brooke Shields' sitcom vehicle *Suddenly Susan*, as magazine owner Jack Richmond, has perked his profile right up.

As the third Brat Packer of beyond-reproach lineage (i.e. in both *Elmo's* and *Club*), Ally Sheedy saw her career take a dive in parallel to Judd Nelson's. Some say smartening up her hair contributed to her downfall, but it's clear the real reason was doing one terrible movie after another. It wasn't until 1998 – 13 years after the Brats' apotheosis – that Sheedy got her name on a decent credit sequence: Lisa Cholodenko's independent movie *High Art*, in which Sheedy plays a photographer recovering from pill addiction.

But no one had further to fall than Molly Ringwald, who transparently and publicly failed to negotiate a transition away from the high-school roles that made her a national icon. After *The Pick-Up Artist* and *King Lear* came films like *Betsy's Wedding* (1990) – Molly gets married. By the turn of the decade, Ringwald was appearing opposite Robert Lindsay in *Strike it Rich*. Say no more. A decade of nothing movies followed, plus a short-lived television sitcom called *Townies*, until she popped up on Hollywood radar with a small role in Kevin '*Scream*' Williamson's directorial debut, *Killing Mrs Tingle* (1999). Unfortunately, that movie's release was eviscerated by America's grief over the Columbine high-school shootings and, tireless promoter of *The Breakfast Club* though he is, Williamson couldn't pull off any Travolta-style renaissance for Ringwald.

Anthony Michael Hall managed to prolong his first tranche of stardom for longer than most of the Brat Pack, *Weird Science* having proved nothing apart from the fact that his lisp-voiced charm was fast disappearing. He played a football star in *Johnny Be Goode*, but put his bulked-up physique to best use in *Edward Scissorhands* (1990), as Winona Ryder's thuggish boyfriend Jim. Another movie of substance, *Six Degrees of Separation* (1993) came his way, but Hall was no longer playing leads. The next year, 1994, he even directed a movie, *Hail Caesar*. It bombed. Five years of virtual anonymity and television guest slots followed, until in 1999 he appeared in a high-profile television movie about computer industry infighting, called *Pirates of Silicon Valley*. Hall played Bill Gates. The Geek had grown up.

Of the male Brats, it was Andrew McCarthy, with three stand-up successes to his name, who had arguably achieved the most in the 80s golden years. It also looked for a while like he was the best bet to carry on in the same vein. After *Fresh Horses*, McCarthy starred in the surprise hit *Weekend at Bernie's* (1989) and nipped across to France to appear in Claude Chabrol's thriller *Docteur M* (1990). But in between then and the *Weekend at Bernie's* sequel, McCarthy's career began its inexorable slide. He got his share of lead roles – *Year of the Gun* (1991), *Only You* (1992), *Night of the Running Man* (1994) – but none of the movies made a splash. In the ones that did – *Mrs Parker and the Vicious Circle* (1994) for instance, where McCarthy played husband Eddie – McCarthy came on like a solid character actor, and slowly his star status ebbed. The 1997 movie *Stag* might have paid off – unfortunately, McCarthy was eclipsed by another comeback kid, Christian Slater, in *Very Bad Things*, another stag-party-goes-wrong movie of similar vintage. But he's still plugging away.

As is Ralph Macchio, the kid who quit the Brat Pack for the *Karate Kid* franchise. His last *KK* movie was in 1989; he popped up in *My Cousin Vinny* (1992) as a mistaken-identity murder defendant (he's the one with the cousin), but has little else of note on his CV.

Matt Dillon was another quitter of the Brat Pack oeuvre, preferring to channel his chiselled cheekbones into sunny comedy (*The Flamingo Kid*, 1984) and dubious psychodrama (*Rebel*, 1985). By the end of the 80s he was already staging a comeback, in Gus Van Sant's pill-popping road movie *Drugstore Cowboy*. A string of respectable, even distinguished, roles followed through the 1990s – Cameron Crowe's grunge homage *Singles* (1992), plight-of-the-homeless fable *The Saint of Fort Washington* (1993), a hapless husband in *To Die For* (1995), another Van Sant project. *Nothing* set the US box-office on fire, until 1998 – Dillon took lead roles in John McNaughton's glistening, intricate thriller *Wild Things* and the Farrelly brothers' monster hit *There's Something About Mary*.

Sean Penn likewise sustained a fine post-Brat Pack run. In fact, his contribution to actual Brat Pack cinema – aside from *Fast Times at Ridgemont High* – was fairly negligible, being more celebrated during the 80s for involvement in flops like *Shanghai Surprise* and *Colors*. In the 1990s his career flourished: graduating to a superb supporting role in Brian De Palma's *Carlito's Way* (1993) and receiving an Oscar nomination for *Dead Man Walking* (1995). Since then, Penn has established himself as one of America's leading actors, with *U Turn* (1997), *The Game* (1997) and, most recently, Woody Allen's *Sweet and Lowdown* (1999), for which he received another Oscar nomination.

Of all the Brat Pack, however, the most unlikely to have made a success of himself is undoubtedly Robert Downey Jr. In and out of jail, rehab and counselling, it's an achievement to have found the time to do any acting at all. But not only did Downey manage to survive the bombs that downed fellow Brat Packers (*The Pick-Up Artist*, *Johnny Be Goode*), he flourished alongside Mel Gibson in *Air America* (1990), performed seamlessly in *Chaplin* (1992) and sweated efficiently in the service of *Natural Born Killers* (1994). He also earned the admiration and loyalty of a raft of name directors: Robert Altman cast him in *Short Cuts* (1993) and *The Gingerbread Man* (1997), Mike Figgis in *One Night Stand* (1996) and Neil Jordan in *In Dreams* (1999). James Toback came in to help out with *Two Girls and a Guy* (1997) and *Black and White* (1999). Truly, a knock-back to all those cautionary tales we've heard all our lives.

The two jewels in the crown of the Brat Pack hardly need much updating, however, since their subsequent careers are essential fodder for the celebrity carousel that the Brat Pack themselves virtually initiated. Demi Moore put deep water between herself and the rest of the Pack by starring in *Ghost* (1990), a massive box-office success that benefited her more than luckless co-star Patrick Swayze. Thereafter, *Indecent Proposal* (1993) and *Disclosure* (1994) focussed attention on Moore the well-honed bod, turning her into a major A-List star in the process. Since then it's been hit and miss – *Striptease* (1996) occasioned much ridicule, but *GI Jane* (1997) saw an impressive abundance of crop-headed toughness. Lately, she's attempted to 'stretch' – Belgian director Alain Berliner cast her in *Passion of Mind*, and she played an over-religious Jew in *Deconstructing Harry* (1997) for Woody Allen.

But the one who's won, the Brattiest Brat of them all, is Tom Cruise. The Cruiser is by some distance the planet's most successful film star, combining machine-tooled box-office hits with not-unimpressive acting jobs of considerable accomplishment. Right from the start, Cruise sought out directors and co-stars of talent, and the hits kept on coming. The same year, 1986, saw the strategy triumph – a glossy, button-pushing action hit *Top Gun* and a never-mind-the-width-feel-the-quality partnership with Paul Newman and Martin Scorsese for *The Color of Money*. There have been wobbles (*Days of Thunder*, *Far and Away*), but for every *Cocktail* (1988), there's a *Rain Man* (1988); for every *Mission: Impossible* (1996), there's a *Jerry Maguire* (1996). And the Cruise juggernaut doesn't look like stopping any time soon, even if it is slowing down – the interminable production of first *Eyes Wide Shut* (1999) and then *Mission: Impossible 2* (2000) have restricted Cruise's screen appearances in the late 90s.

The New Teen Generation

The Brat Pack didn't invent the idea of celebrity lifestyle, but they were the first group of film stars to live out their formative years in the media spotlight *without* the guiding hand of the Hollywood studio system to mask their indiscretions and soften their embarrassments. In any case, behaving badly was what the 80s in many ways was all about. Ironic, then, that the mid-90s saw the rise of a new generation of teen stars, performing in their own wave of teen movies. This time around, however, the mood and attitude was entirely different: these are performers who are following a career game-plan and whose looks and opinions are carefully sculpted by experts.

Who are this new generation, this new pack of brats? As yet, there are few defining movies, nothing in the way of easily identifiable connections that bind a group together. Names proliferate as we speak, with no end in sight. There are special cases, predecessors, antecedents of the New Brats – Drew '*ET*' Barrymore, Christina 'Wednesday Addams' Ricci, Edward '*T2*' Furlong. Fine actors though they are, they don't owe their celebrity to the teen revival. Senior members of this generation are Sarah Michelle Gellar, Reese Witherspoon, Denise Williams, Ryan Phillippe, Neve Campbell, Freddie Prinze Jr, Clare Danes and Jennifer Love Hewitt. Coming up fast on the rails are Jason Schwartzman, Mena Suvari, Jared Leto, Heath Ledger, Natasha Lyonne, James van Der Beek, Katie Holmes, Rachael Leigh Cook and Julia Stiles. Hanging in there and hoping for better things are Casper van Dien, Scott Wolf, Brendan Sexton III, Alyssa Milano, Claire Forlani, Devon Sawa, Ali Larter and Selma Blair.

This is an unprecedented outburst of tyro talent, and one that will undoubtedly take a cruel toll in the years ahead. The names above are only a few of the as-yet-unlined faces that are thronging casting sessions and badgering acting coaches in contemporary Hollywood. Only time will tell which of these bright young things will carve themselves a substantial career, and which will drop down the credit lists and fill out the guest-star slots on mediocre television shows. Right now, though, Hollywood is enjoying itself – gorging, as it were, on fresh meat that seems in endless supply. One day, of course, we'll look back on these people and wonder, like we did about the Brat Pack, where it all went.

But that's the future. For now, it's enough to look for the New Brats' answer to *The Outsiders*. Two films acted as template-setters – equivalents, if you will, of *Halloween* and *Fast Times at Ridgemont High*. On the side of the devil we have *Scream*, the Wes Craven movie released at Christmas 1996, that via its smarty-pants Kevin Williamson script, allowed for the evisceration of good-looking high-schoolers who appeared very much to appreciate the rules of the slasher movie they were involved in. It's no accident that *Scream* picked off-the-rails icon Drew Barrymore to be the first victim of its game-playing killer. Holding the fort for love and romance was *Clueless*, released in the summer of 1995, which had Alicia Silverstone as a Beverly Hills rich kid going through the motions of Jane Austen's Emma, trying to fix up marriages for her friends and finding one herself.

But these were the harbingers. When the film history of the period is written, one film will be seen to have drawn together a group of newly-minted actors, barely heard of before. That film is *I Know What You Did Last Summer*. Based, like *The Outsiders*, on a novel (written in 1975 by Lois Duncan), *I Know What You Did Last Summer* was rushed into production to capitalise on the success that *Scream* had enjoyed. The same script-writer, Kevin Williamson, was employed, but *I Know What You Did Last Summer* was a much more straightforward affair. Its makers thought so little of it on its commencement that it was entrusted to a little-known Scottish director, Jim Gillespie, who was best known for the British television series *Ghostbusters of East Finchley*. But again like *The Outsiders*, its cast will ensure it its place in history.

There were four of them: Sarah Michelle Gellar, Jennifer Love Hewitt, Ryan Phillippe and Freddie Prinze Jr. The plot was simple and urban-myth-orientated: four teens run down a man dressed in fishing gear, and leave the body; a year later, a note arrives emblazoned with the titular phrase, and a mysterious oilskin-clad killer starts laying about him with a gutting hook. Released in October 1997, *I Know What You Did Last Summer* netted over $70m.

The plethora of teen-oriented television series that packed US airwaves during the mid-1990s was, in retrospect, the forcing ground for the New Brats. Both Hewitt and Gellar had made their mark in television: Hewitt on *Party of Five*, a show about a family living without parents, and Gellar in *Buffy the Vampire Slayer*, itself a small-screen version of a movie that had trailed unsuccessfully in the wake of the teen movie surge first time around, back in 1992. Another graduate of *Party of Five*, Neve Campbell, had already turned herself into a major star in *Scream* and a teen witch film called *The Craft*. Claire Danes had graduated from *My So Called Life*, an acclaimed but swiftly cancelled series, to playing Juliet to Leonardo DiCaprio's Romeo in Baz Luhrman's Shakespeare adaptation.

Once this particular door was opened, it became an unstoppable flood. Participation in *Dawson's Creek*, a television series dreamed up by that man Kevin Williamson, practically guaranteed a big-screen career: Katie Holmes starred in *Go* and *Disturbing Behaviour*; James Van Der Beek made *Varsity Blues*; Michelle Williams went for *Halloween: H20*; Joshua Jackson graduated to *Cruel Intentions* and *The Skulls*. Other television faces joined in the scramble. Melissa Joan Hart went from television series *Sabrina the Teenage Witch* to the movie *Drive Me Crazy*. (As if to confirm her claim as the successor to Alicia Silverstone, Hart is also starring in the television series spin-off from *Clueless*.) Jared Leto, fresh from *My So-Called Life*, did the teen horror thing in *Urban Legend*, then forged upwards and onwards to *Fight Club*, *American Psycho* and *Requiem for a Dream*.

The list goes on and on.

Some of the New Brats have, on the other hand, proved themselves in the movies. Both Phillippe and Prinze started out with small parts on television (Phillippe in the long-running daytime soap *One Life to Live*; Prinze a four-line role in another, *Family Matters*). But Phillippe advanced by getting one of the shipboard roles in Ridley Scott's *White Squall*, and Prinze got to kiss Claire Danes in the otherwise undistinguished *To Gillian on her 37th Birthday*.

But it was after *I Know What You Did Last Summer* that the teen blizzard came thick and fast. Phillippe and Gellar hooked up again for *Cruel Intentions*. Hewitt spent 1997 and 1998 doing *I Still Know What You Did Last Summer* and *Can't Hardly Wait*. Prinze floated off to do *Wing Commander* and *She's All That*. And this is merely the tip of the iceberg.

At this early stage, only three years into the phenomenon, analysis of new teen movie uncovers a number of strands operating in parallel. Taking its cue from the *Scream/I Know What You Did Last Summer* phenomenon, we have a revival of the teen horror phenomenon. Thus we have *I Still Know...*, *Urban Legend* (in which a campus killer appears to be working through hoary 'urban myths'), *The Faculty* (a *Breakfast Club* meets *Invasion of the Bodysnatchers* story, scripted by, yes, Kevin Williamson), *Halloween: H20* (a seventh, 20th-anniversary instalment of the original teen slasher), *Killing Mrs Tingle* (a teacher-hostage thriller directed by, yes, Kevin Williamson) and *Final Destination* (a string of teen deaths that appear ordained by fate).

All these movies reflect the knowingness that *Scream* introduced into the teen horror genre. The originals, like *Halloween* and *A Nightmare on Elm Street*, responded to the iron inevitability of folk legend or dream logic; the new batch all factor in a sense of the inescapability of destiny, an appreciation of the rules of the game. In *Scream*, the teens know they're in a horror movie; in *The Faculty*, they have no trouble in suspecting their teachers are aliens; in *Urban Legend*, they all know the urban legends. This all makes for a curiously febrile, nervously witty form of horror, where the emphasis isn't on gore, or even the ingenuity with which one hapless teen after another is despatched. It's actually strangely literary in quality, where narrative is in charge and is expected to control events.

It shouldn't be a surprise, therefore, that the second strand of New Brat movies should involve a close relationship with the most powerful literary models around. Following in the wake of *Clueless*, and the teened-up adaptation of *Romeo and Juliet* starring DiCaprio and Danes, we witnessed a surge of teen rewrites of storybook classics of yesteryear. Thus, *Les Liaisons Dangereuses* became *Cruel Intentions*, with Sarah Michelle Gellar in the scheming Madame Merteuil role and Ryan Phillippe doing Valmont; *She's All That* took its cue from *Pygmalion*; *10 Things I Hate About You* updated *The Taming of the Shrew*; *Crime and Punishment in Suburbia* (starring yet another Dawson's Creek alumnus, Monica Keener), reworks the Dostoyevsky novel. On one level, these movies bag an audience because they're based on the very books high-schoolers would be studying in their literature seminars. Even if this clutch of movies doesn't always rise to the occasion, on another level they assuredly seek to affirm the strength of the literary models they're imitating.

The third category of New Brat movies we can identify is the simplest: the straight teen movie. Far ahead of the pack is our generation's answer to *Porky's* – *American Pie*. A huge financial success, *Pie* offered a mildly updated version of the perennial teen theme of Losin' It. Four male high-schoolers have the prom coming up, and make a bet to get some action by then. Instead of shower-room voyeurism, we have internet link-up. That's something of an advance. Another big hitter for the New Brats was *Starship Troopers*, an incredibly violent sci-fi thriller from Paul '*Robocop*' Verhoeven. Verhoeven specialises in a distinctive brand of luridly coloured irony, and *Starship Troopers* was a perfect vehicle for the chisel-jawed and fine-cheekboned performers required. Denise Richards and Patrick Muldoon were scooped from *Melrose Place*, Casper Van Dien and Dina Meyer from *Beverly Hills 90210*; Verhoeven had them playing totally straight in a thin-line-treading satire on paranoid totalitarianism. Two more solid hits came in the shape of *Varsity Blues*, an old-fashioned football yarn starring James van der Beek, and *Never Been Kissed*, a literally revisionist high-school tale in which Drew Barrymore gets to revisit her classroom days as an undercover reporter working on a story. Yet another circle is closed here: it was precisely the same mission that fresh-faced journalist Cameron Crowe undertook two decades earlier, and produced the text that would become teen movie *Fast Times at Ridgemont High*. *Election*, sadly, wasn't a financial success, despite the fine performance of Reese Witherspoon as an iron-hard high-schooler running for class president, and the presence of teen icon Matthew Broderick as a teacher with a love–hate fascination for his star pupil.

The fourth kind of teen movie spawned in this current New Brat outpouring is, for want of a better phrase, the art teen movie. Gregg Araki, the director of plasticky LA fables like *The Doom Generation* and *Totally F***ed Up*, showed prescience, if nothing else, in corralling teen faces like Mena Suvari, Ryan Phillippe, Denise Richards and Scott 'son of James' Caan for his plasticky LA fable *Nowhere*, which came out in 1997. The mainstream teen audience, however, was unlikely to go anywhere near an Araki film, and so it proved. *Go*, on the other hand, was a more calculated attempt to lure the high-minded end of the teen audience. Directed by Doug Liman, who had masterminded the surprise success of *Swingers*, *Go* aped the elaborate flashback structure of *Pulp Fiction*, while focusing on the rarely examined American rave scene. Katie Holmes (*Dawson's Creek*) and Scott Wolf (*Party of Five*) climbed on board, as did Britain's own Desmond Askew, once of *Grange Hill*. *Slums of Beverly Hills* put the case for the embitterment of the adolescent female, with Natasha Lyonne following up her role as Woody Allen's alter ego in *Everyone Says I Love You*. *Rushmore*, finally, is the art teen-movie masterpiece, a genuinely unclassifiable original about an ultra-keen student, named Max Fischer, who falls in love with a teacher. Max is played by Jason Schwartzman, the nephew of Francis Ford Coppola, who kicked the whole Brat Pack thing off in the first place. Another circle closed.

This survey can only skim the surface of the 90s teen revival, but already the evidence is that it's at least the equal of the original teen movie wave in its diversity and marketability. What's markedly different, however, is that the New Brats are not much of a Pack – at least, not yet. Where 10 or 15 names in the 80s dominated the teen movies of the time, several dozen are regularly interchanged in the late 90s. Of course, in 20 years time, marginal figures are likely to have been sloughed off and filmgoers will be left with a handful of semi-permanent names to conjure with. Just like the real Brat Pack.

The difference, in the current generation, is that actors are considerably more professional – in the sense of being coached, strategised and planned. Take, as an example, teen fantasy icon Denise Richards. Richards started out modelling in catalogues while still at high school in San Diego. She started working the audition circuit shortly afterwards. Early jobs were spots as eye candy on shows like *Saved by the Bell* and *Married… with Children*, and a legendary *Seinfeld* episode where her cleavage distracts George Costanza in the middle of a meeting with her father, an NBC executive. She auditioned for *Showgirls*, but didn't get cast; Paul Verhoeven remembered her, however, and cast her in his next film, which turned out to be *Starship Troopers*. Since then she's switched between studio films – the blood-heat thriller *Wild Things*, for Columbia, and MGM's *The World is Not Enough* – and snappy independents, like the beauty pageant satire *Drop Dead Gorgeous*. According to casting director John Papsidera, who cast her in *Drop Dead Gorgeous*: "It's a real team effort. Her agent, Chuck James at Gersh, has been an integral part of planning and designing the kind of projects that they want to target."

As if the New Brats couldn't get any more self-conscious over their careers, then consider this. In November 1996, American *Esquire* magazine parodied Hollywood's manic feeding frenzy for hot young talent by parading a spoof cover story about a young actress called Allegra Coleman ('Hollywood's Next Dream Girl'). Written by Martha Sherrill, the article aped entertainment-industry puff pieces by describing the fictitious Coleman's acting abilities, hinting at a romance with David Schwimmer and including fulsome praise from celebrity fans. The woman used as the subject for the cover picture was a model called Ali Larter. Naturally, *Esquire* magazine was the recipient of frantic phone calls from Hollywood talent scouts after the article came out, but the real twist is this: Larter has got a proper career as a New Brat movie actress out of the scam, with roles in *Varsity Blues*, *Drive Me Crazy* and *Final Destination*. The teen movie revival began with successful attempts to recycle what had gone before; and now, like *Weird Science*, Hollywood is finding star material in its own fictitious creations. You couldn't make it up.

THE PLAYERS by Steven Davies

MATTHEW BRODERICK
Born 21 March 1962
New York City

Matthew Broderick starred in two of the most commercially successful teen films of the 80s – *WarGames* (1983) and *Ferris Bueller's Day Off* (1986). Sidney Lumet, who directed Broderick in *Family Business* (1989) called him "one of the two best young actors in the United States. There's just this profundity to his work that you rarely, if ever, see in actors that young. He's totally involved, and he's incapable of being a cliché."

Although Broderick was only 19 when he made his first feature film appearance, he had already made a name for himself on stage, having developed a working relationship with the playwrights Horton Foote and Neil Simon. Broderick's actor father James (*Dog Day Afternoon*, *Five Easy Pieces*) had originally got his son a part in a play when he was just eight years old, but Broderick junior was having none of it: "The idea of actually going on the stage scared me so much that I started crying. I thought I didn't want to be an actor after that, and I didn't get back into it until high school."

At Walden school in Manhattan, Broderick auditioned for a small part in *A Midsummer Night's Dream* and got it. He then went on to appear in 10 more plays. After graduating, he made his professional stage debut in 1979 in an off-off-Broadway production of Foote's *On Valentine's Day* with his father, James Broderick, in the lead. His performance resulted in a lead role offer for the film *No Small Affair*, about a teenager obsessed with an cabaret singer. He was set to co-star with Sally Field and be directed by Martin Ritt. But, after creative differences (nothing to do with Broderick), the film fell through. It was later made by Jerry Schatzberg with Jon Cryer and Demi Moore in the lead roles.

For a while, no more film offers came along, despite Broderick attending dozens of auditions. He even accepted a commercial for an anti-itch cream! Then, although his agent advised against it, Broderick took the role of David, a confused teenager, in Harvey Fierstein's gay play, *Torch Song Trilogy*. Fierstein was also in the play as a drag queen called Arnold Beckoff, who looks after the Broderick character. Although based in a minor New York theatre, the play was a success and Broderick won rave reviews: "Matthew Broderick gives one of the most original, witty and touching performances I've ever seen from a young actor" (*Newsweek*). The play moved to a bigger theatre and Broderick won the Outer Critics' Circle and Village awards for his performance.

In the audience one night was the film director, Herbert Ross, who was himself busier than ever, at the time both directing Neil Simon's play *Brighton Beach Memoirs* and his own film version of Simon's *Max Dugan Returns* (1982), with Jason Robards, Donald Sutherland and Marsha Mason. Ross asked Broderick to audition and at the end of the day, the casting director informed a delighted Broderick he'd landed both parts. He was a 20-year old actor about to embark on playing two 15-year-old characters. In *Brighton Beach Memoirs* his performance as the teenager Eugene Morris Jerome won him a Tony award.

However, fresh-faced Broderick made a huge impact in John Badham's *WarGames*, a suspenseful, cautionary political satire. . At the time of its release, reports began to appear discussing the possibility of the scenario happening for real. "Could It Ever Happen?" asked Richard Halloran in The New York Times. "No!" stressed Washington officials. Perhaps they were forgetting an incident which happened a year earlier. A few clever Manhattan students used their computer to scramble the entire Canadian banking system for several days, while a group of other bright sparks entered the computer system of a major hospital complex, rearranging patients' records.

Broderick followed up *WarGames* with more stage work and an appearance in the film version of Horton Foote's *1918* (1985), as Brother Vaughn, a restless teen from Texas. He took the part as a tribute to his father (who had a leading role in the original stage production). James Broderick died on 1 November 1982 aged 55, just before his son hit the big time with *WarGames*.

Next, Broderick was the young thief in constant contact with God, Philippe the Mouse in *Ladyhawke* (1985), a medieval fantasy about a knight and his lover (Rutger Jauer and Michelle Pfieffer) afflicted by a strange curse. Broderick also starred in a television edition of Athol Fugard's *Master Harold… and the Boys* (1985) and a video version of *Cinderella* (1985), and he recreated his role as Brother Vaughn for *On Valentine's Day* (1986), Horton Foote's prequel to *1918*.

However, the perennially boyish Broderick achieved world-wide fame and popularity at the age of 24, passing for a 16-year-old rich-kid high-schooler in *Ferris Bueller's Day Off* (1986). The film was extremely popular at the box-office and spawned a television sitcom spin-off (with Charlie Schlatter in the Broderick role and Jennifer Anniston as his sister, Jeannie).

By the end of 1986, Broderick was topping popularity polls, beating Harrison Ford and Michael Douglas: "When I started out, looking so young was a definite advantage. At the time there were so many good teenage roles about and though I was no longer a teenager, I would've hated to miss out on a part like Ferris," he commented.

Ferris also introduced Broderick to Jennifer Grey, who played his sister Jeanie, and the pair dated for three years.

In *Project X* (1987), Broderick co-starred with his future girlfriend, Helen Hunt. He played an Air Force pilot engaged in secret research with lab chimps who has to decide where his principles lie when he realises his endearing new friends will be disposable once the project is complete. Unfortunately for Broderick, the chimps, especially Willie, steal the show.

After another off-Broadway stint in Horton Foote's *The Widow Claire*, he was back as Eugene Morris Jerome in the film version of *Biloxi Blues*, the second part of Neil Simon's autobiographical trilogy. This time, Eugene is taken from Brooklyn to a Mississippi army boot camp. Enlisting for a gruelling 10 weeks of basic training, he meets adult life head-on, but even his introduction to prejudice, sex and bunkhouse humour can't prepare him for his first meeting with his psychotic drill sergeant (Christopher Walken). Broderick delivers another solid performance, but is pretty vacant as the film's narrator.

Biloxi Blues was a hit, but soon after the film was completed, Broderick had more serious matters to contend with. In August 1987, Broderick and Jennifer Grey were involved in a terrifying car crash while holidaying in Ireland. Their BMW collided with a Volvo, killing both occupants – a 28 year-old man and his 63-year-old mother. Apart from a few broken ribs, Broderick was OK, as was Grey who escaped with minor bruising. Broderick faced a five-year prison sentence after admitting he may have been driving on the wrong side of the road. In February 1988, he pleaded guilty to careless driving, but received only a fine of £100. "FERRIS BUELLER'S LET OFF" was the headline in *The New York Post*. The actor spent a year in therapy.

At the end of 1988, Broderick took a supporting role in the film adaptation of *Torch Song Trilogy*, as Alan, the gay partner of drag queen Arnold Beckoff, again played by Harvey Fierstein. Next, Broderick played Dustin Hoffman's son and Sean Connery's grandson in Sidney Lumet's comedy-drama, *Family Business* (1989) and followed it up with a sparkling performance as a New York film student who delivers exotic animals to a floating restaurant in Andrew Bergman's *The Freshman* (1990). It's a glorious spoof of all the Mob movies you ever saw, with Marlon Brando larger than life in a delicious parody of his Godfather character.

Then, in *Glory* (1990), sporting a moustache and goatee, Broderick played a colonel called Robert Gould who lead the first platoon of blacks during the American Civil War. The film was a triple-Oscar winner, although Broderick was left without a gong. He then waited two years before his next film role, as a yuppie, in the awful comedy *Out on a Limb* (1992). Broderick should have waited a bit longer . The film bombed. (*Variety* named it worst film of the year).

The rest of the 90s was hit and miss for the baby-faced beau – who doesn't seem to have aged since *Ferris Bueller's Day Off*. Many parts were only supporting roles – *Cider House Rules* (1993) and *Mrs Parker and the Vicious Circle* (1994). His directorial debut *Infinity* (1996) (scripted by his mother) didn't fare too well at the box office, although he kept his profile high by appearing with Anthony Hopkins in Alan Parker's *The Road to Welville* (1994) and with Jim Carrey in *The Cable Guy* (1996). However, Broderick found his biggest audience as the voice of Simba in Disney's *The Lion King* (1994).

More recently, Broderick releases such as *Godzilla* (1998) and the big-budget extravaganza *Inspector Gadget* (1999) failed to set the box office alight. He is, however, still happily married to *Sex in the City* star Sarah Jessica Parker.

TOM CRUISE
(Thomas Cruise Mapother IV)
Born 3 July 1962
Syracuse, New York

While most of the Brat Pack came and went, Tom Cruise succeeded in his mission to become an international movie megastar. According to the British film director David Puttnam, Cruise has more 'want to be' about him than any other American film star – "men want to be him; women simply want him." He is the most successful movie star of his generation.

Christened Thomas Cruise Mapother IV, he was born into a family that moved around a lot while his father looked for work. Cruise's parents later split when he was still young. His father then died of cancer in 1984. "I grew up surrounded by women – my mother and my three sisters," he explains. "So if I ever spoke out of turn or treated a woman in a bad way, I would not be in good shape today! My whole perspective was from seeing how men treated women."

Originally, Cruise planned to become a priest and even spent a year in a Franciscan seminary. Later, a knee injury crushed his hopes of a career in athletics and led to him taking an interest in acting. He appeared in a few school plays, but skipped the traditional stage-school route after an agent got him television work. The television parts were not spectacular, but Cruise had only just left school and he was at least getting some attention.

His debut on the big screen came in Franco Zeffirelli's 1981 rendition of Scott Spencer's novel *Endless Love*. Cruise only had a minor role, 18th-billed, as Billy, but obviously appealed enough to land a more substantial role in *Taps* (1981), which takes a critical look at military school education. Students at the academy go all out to save it from being sold and converted into a block of condominiums. Cruise, as headstrong David Shawn, one of the crew-cut cadets, plays a big part in the ensuing bloodbath and his character is more memorable than the two leads (Timothy Hutton and Sean Penn), who seem far too nice to be involved with machine guns.

Cruise didn't have much to do in Coppola's *The Outsiders* (1983), clearly outshone by Matt Dillon and C Thomas Howell, but he landed star billing in *Losin' It* (1983), a comedy in which he loses his virginity to Shelley Long. Then, later in 1983, came Paul Brickman's more satirical effort *Risky Business,* which starred Cruise as Joel Goodson, a good student growing up in Chicago's posh suburbs, who goes off the rails while his parents are away. Nancy Klopper, the casting director on *Risky Business* believes Cruise was always way ahead of the other Brat Packers: "He soared on his own from the very beginning. I have only the warmest of feelings for Tom as he's remained the same thoughtful, warm and dedicated young man that he was when I met him in 1981."

Undoubtedly Cruise's big break, *Risky Business*, which grossed $65 million in the USA, presented him as the perfect all-American pin-up boy for the 80s. Tom stripped down to his underwear for pretty hooker Rebecca DeMornay, and the rest is history.

However, Cruise did do one more youth movie, *All The Right Moves,* in which he plays an ambitious high-school athlete who tries to win a scholarship to escape his small-town existence. The film was a hit and Cruise was a star. By this point, he was even dating Rebecca DeMornay. However, *Legend* (1985), Ridley Scott's embarrassing fairy tale about unicorns, didn't exactly help Cruise's career storm forward, although as a fantasy hero in green tights, he was at least no longer playing high-school teenagers. On his return from Britain he split up from Rebecca DeMornay.

Cruise leapt from teen heart-throb to bona fide movie star in the number one hit of 1986, *Top Gun*. *Top Gun* is a producer's movie – Don Simpson and Jerry Bruckheimer's portrait of the young macho 80s audience's self-image. Not surprisingly, the film grossed over $150 million and recruitment into the Navy really did soar. In 1986 and 1987, Cruise was listed as the number one box-office draw in the United States, beating the likes of Clint Eastwood, Sylvester Stallone and Eddie Murphy. In May 1987, he married the actress Mimi Rogers.

The next stage of the Cruise strategy was getting to appear with higher profile names. Indeed, his international success is in part down to the fact he managed to work with noted directors and highly rated older actors. The usual scenario of a coming-of-age Cruise taken in hand by a father figure meant he could always get away with appearing with screen legends. Paul Newman taught him how to be a pool shark in Martin Scorsese's sequel to *The Hustler*, *The Color of Money* (Cruise flashed his smile a lot, Newman got an Oscar) and Dustin Hoffman softened his detached, uncaring character in Barry Levinson's *Rain Man* (1988). The latter role was a demanding one for Cruise, which saw him slowly building a relationship with the autistic savant brother he never knew he had. *Rain Man* was showered with Oscars, although Cruise was again left out. But he had won the friendship of Hollywood's main players. Paul Newman described him as "the next Hollywood legend", while Dustin Hoffman called him "the biggest star in the world".

The more mature assignments were interspersed with more commercial films including *Cocktail* (1988), which had Cruise as Brian Flanagan, a student who gets a job in an Upper East Side bar and is taught to make good cocktails by yet another father figure, Bryan Brown. As well as mixing Manhattans in Manhattan and flirting with beautiful, wealthy women, he also learns that love is indeed worth more than money. *Days of Thunder* (1990) was *Top Gun* on wheels . Nevertheless, all of these projects helped enlarge the Cruise name – literally. The publicity for *Days of Thunder* put his name not only above the title, but in letters four times as large.

Cruise ditched his grin for one film, Oliver Stone's *Born on the Fourth of July* (1989). His performance as the paraplegic Vietnam veteran Ron Kovic won him a Golden Globe Award and an Oscar nomination, convincing many critics he could act as well as smile.

In 1990, Cruise changed wives. His three-year marriage to actress Mimi Rogers ended and he married his *Days of Thunder* co-star, Australian actress Nicole Kidman. The ceremony took place in secret, in Telluride, Colorado, on Christmas Eve. By this time, Cruise had few rivals in the realm of glamorous A-list leading men. *A Few Good Men* (1992) and *The Firm* (1993) were box-office hits, as was the action-by-numbers pic *Mission: Impossible* (1996), the first film on which Cruise was credited as a producer. Also in 1996, Cruise won another Golden Globe and a second Oscar nomination for his part in Cameron Crowe's *Jerry Maguire*. Here, Cruise was impressive as the slick sports agent who gets fired from his job and scrambles to get back to the top.

Then, in November 1996, Cruise and wife Nicole Kidman were spotted at the English studio locations for what would be Stanley Kubrick's last film, *Eyes Wide Shut*, described in the original Warner Bros. press release as 'a story of jealousy and sexual obsession'. Eighteen months later, while Kubrick fans debated whether Cruise and Kidman were worthy of working with the greatest living film director, Hollywood's hottest couple were still being recalled for reshoots by the man who was notorious for obsessive perfectionism. Cruise had come a long way from the teen flicks of the early 1980s and working with the celebrated auteur can be seen as the high point of his career.

Nevertheless, his fees are still among the highest in Hollywood and his star is set to shine even brighter. He spent the summer of 1999 shooting the *Mission Impossible* sequel in Sydney, as well as completing *Magnolia*, in which he plays a nasty television guru who plugs seminars teaching insecure men how to seduce women.

There's no denying Cruise has achieved what he set out to do. It's easy to forget he began his career as just another pretty Brat Packer. Now he seems to be riding one of the longest winning streaks in Hollywood history.

MATT DILLON
Born 18 February 1964
New Rochelle, New York

Born in a posh New York suburb, New Rochelle, and raised in a tight-knit, Irish Catholic family, Matt Dillon was the second oldest of five boys and a girl. His dad Paul was a stockbroker, while mum Mary Ellen looked after the home and kids. One of Dillon's brothers, Kevin, followed him into the acting profession, appearing in such films as *Platoon*, *The Doors* and *The Blob*.

Matt Dillon caught the acting bug after appearing as Benjamin Franklin in a school play in the fourth grade. He was a pupil at Larchmiont's Hommocks Junior High when at 14 years of age, while he was dodging maths class, some talent scouts spotted him. They had been sent to the school by the casting director Vic Ramos, who was searching for 'realistic types' with no previous acting experience for a new low-budget film. After school, Dillon told his mum he'd been asked to attend an interview with Ramos about a film being made by some brothers. Later, of course, she found out he was referring to Warner Bros.

According to Ramos, who went on to become Dillon's long-time manager, when he arrived at his Manhattan office for the interview, Dillon looked at the suits and asked, "Do I get my car fare back?" He then lit a cigarette and told them, "I'm a thief and I'm working up some robbery schemes." The interviewers asked the young schoolboy what his parents did. "My dad's a fucking stockbroker. My mum don't do shit." Realising he was going too far, he then backtracked and said, "I mean, she's a housewife – no profession… No offence."

One of the interviewers was the director Jonathan Kaplan, who described what he saw as "a working class, Lower East Side, Italian pose from a middle-class Irish kid from the suburbs." Both he and Ramos decided they wanted Dillon to play Richie White, the delinquent teen whose death sparks gang violence in *Over the Edge*. Orion Pictures originally planned to release the film in 1979, but it was withheld for more than a year after poor test screenings and a general fear that it would incite real life riots. But Dillon's performance was impressive for an actor so young and it was his moody good looks that caught the attention of casting directors. Movie roles came thick and fast, forcing Dillon to quit school in the 11th grade. But the films played on his pretty face rather than his acting ability. In *Little Darlings* (1980) he played Randy, the young stud of a summer camp, while in *My Bodyguard* (1980) he was the bully of a Chicago high school. However, in Dillon's physical appearance, there is much more than beauty. He has an interesting face with a James Dean-style persona. Unlike the Rob Lowes of this world, Dillon can show a real range of expression. As the school gang leader in *My Bodyguard*, he is far more menacing than Lowe is in a similar sinister role in *Bad Influence*.

In *Liar's Moon* (1981), he was the poor boy love interest of wealthy beauty Cindy Fisher with whom he elopes despite parental opposition. Interestingly, this latter film by David Fisher was shot with two different endings, both of which were released. Following a role in a PBS television movie, *The Great American Fourth of July and Other Disasters*, came perhaps the best example of Dillon's acting ability in *Tex* (1982), the first in his SE Hinton trilogy. In Tim Hunter's film, Dillon plays another troubled teen loner, Tex McCormick, brilliantly inflecting an insecure, vulnerable persona.

By this point, his manager Vic Ramos had made sure his client's face was regularly appearing in glossy teen magazines. Dillon had become a bona fide teen idol with his own fan club (and sackfuls of mail from adoring female fans). But even during these years as a heart-throb, critics had already singled out Dillon from his fellow pin-ups Rob Lowe and Ralph Macchio as a real actor.

After befriending the author Susan (SE) Hinton on the set of *Tex*, Dillon secured the role of Dallas Winston in Francis Ford Coppola's adaptation of Hinton's novel *The Outsiders* (1983). Dillon appears to even better effect in Coppola's next film, *Rumble Fish* (1983), which was also shot in Tulsa and made back-to-back with *The Outsiders*. It, too, is based on a novel by Hinton. Coppola's film suffered a similar fate to Alex Cox's *Repo Man*, (1984), another Universal picture made around the same time. Cox blames the failure of both pictures on a regime change: "The head of the studio Bob Rehme was ousted from his post and a new boss came in. The new guy at Universal had to make the person who previously held his chair look bad. So all the films Universal had made were doomed at that point. Some of them, like *Streets of Fire*, which cost $20 million, did get a release in an attempt to recoup. But cheaper films like *Repo Man* and *Rumble Fish* had to be dumped because they pissed off the executives."

Despite the failure of *Rumble Fish* at the box-office, the film was talked about and became something of a cult classic, doing Dillon no harm at all. He won much critical praise for the title role in Garry Marshall's comedy *The Flamingo Kid* (1984). As the naïve student Jeffrey Willis, working at a Long Island beach club, Dillon was good in a comedy role, a marked change from a string of surly youth parts. His move into the mainstream came a year later when he teamed with Gene Hackman for the thriller *Target* (1985). Dillon goes in search of his kidnapped mother and learns along the way that his seemingly average father (Hackman) is an ex-CIA agent. Cue far-fetched car chases and bloodshed.

Things really went awry for Dillon in *Rebel* (1986), in which he played an American deserter from World War Two, who falls in love with a night-club singer in wartime Australia. He was unconvincing in a low-budget Aussie drama. His next few films were just as disastrous. The public stayed away from the version of Richard Wright's novel *Native Son* (1986), as well as *The Big Town* (1987), which had Dillon as a whiz-kid backroom gambler. He teamed up with Andrew McCarthy and played yet another unhinged drifter in *Kansas* (1988). Next came *Bloodhounds of Broadway* (1988) with Dillon as a lousy horse player in a competent adaptation of Damon Runyon's short stories about New Year's Eve on Broadway in 1928 – but the picture was barely released.

With *Drugstore Cowboy* (1989), Dillon finally made the transition from young stud to serious actor, winning rave reviews for his performance as Bob Hughes, a self-confessed 'drug fiend' who robs drugstores, not for money – for drugs. But a brush with death makes Bob realise he must clean up his act if he's not to go the same way. Unfortunately, his junkie wife Diane (Kelly Lynch) refuses to go along with him. Gus Van Sant's film is set in 1971 (before crack) and takes an unclichéd, bleak but unsympathetic look at junkies' meandering lives, without sentiment or criticism. Dillon's performance made this the most talked about independent American film of 1989. A year after its release in Britain, Dillon was also acknowledged by the National Film Theatre in London with a retrospective of his films – unusual for an actor so young.

Unfortunately, Dillon chose to follow up his 1989 success with a remake of the Robert Wagner/Joanne Woodward thriller *A Kiss Before Dying* (1991). In this update of Ira Levin's novel, Dillon is in the Wagner role as Corliss, who tries to think of the best way to dispose of the heiress (Sean Young) with whom he's having an affair. Her twin sister becomes the next target when it becomes clear she may inherit the millions. The film looked like a television movie and next, in the same year, Dillon opted for the real thing, making an appearance in the television three-parter *Women & Men 2: In Love There Are No Rules*, playing a boxer with marital problems.

Dillon was back on track as Cliff Poncier, a wannabe grunge rock star, in Cameron Crowe's *Singles* (1992), a funny romantic comedy which follows the exploits of a group of twentysomethings searching for, and occasionally running from, love. It was a supporting role, but Dillon put in a fine performance.

Following a cameo in Spike Lee's *Malcolm X* (1992), Dillon played Mathew, a homeless schizophrenic in Tim Hunter's *The Saint of Fort Washington* (1993); and a cocky FBI agent in *Golden Gate* (1993). He was impressive in Anthony Minghella's *Mr Wonderful* (1993) as the divorcee who tries to find Mr Right for his ex (Annabella Sciorra) and also impressed critics as Nicole Kidman's husband in the quirky cult film *To Die For* (1995). Then he scored again in Ted Demme's thirtysomething comedy/drama *Beautiful Girls* (1996) as a football star turned snow-plough-driver who can't stop cheating on his girlfriend. He then played a cool surf music star in *Grace of My Heart* (1996), Allison Anders' look at world of 60s pop; and was back as a surly gang leader in *Albino Aligator* (1996), Kevin Spacey's directorial debut about a hold-up gone wrong. In the Frank Oz comedy *In and Out* (1997) he played an actor modelled on Tom Hanks, and landed the starring role in the 1998 thriller *Wild Things*.

As well as his acting career, Dillon's also been dabbling in the restaurant business, buying a New York bar called the Whiskey and a trendy eatery called the Falls, both close to his uptown bachelor pad. And he is a bachelor again having recently ended his three-year relationship with actress Cameron Diaz, who co-starred with him in the schmaltzy 1998 romantic comedy *There's Something About Mary*. Dillon's latest big project was his directorial debut *City of Ghosts*, a thriller set in Southeast Asia that he also scripted, and he's due to co-star with ex-Blondie singer Debbie Harry in the baseball drama *Deuces Wild* (2000), which will chart the story of the Brooklyn Dodgers' highly controversial relocation to Los Angeles in 1958.

ROBERT DOWNEY Jr
Born 4 April 1965
New York City

Robert Downey Jr was one of Hollywood's hip, blow-dried, 80s brat-packers, but in the space of just 10 years, he managed to descend from clean-cut pin-up to gun-toting junkie fuck-up. By 1996, he'd swapped making movies for smack, crack and a .357 Magnum.

Downey made his screen debut at the age of five in his father's independent film *Pound* (1970). Robert Downey Senior is also the director of low-budget anarchic efforts, including the Mel Brooks' comedy *Putney Swope* (1969) and *The Gong Show Movie* (1980). *Pound* is a film about stray dogs, all played by humans, who are waiting to be put down or collected by their owners. The young Downey played a puppy and his first-ever screen line (to a kid playing a Mexican hairless dog) was, "Got any hair on your balls?" He later appeared in his father's films' *Greaser's Palace* (1972), *Jive* (1976) and *Up the Academy* (1980). He smoked his first joint at the age of eight, before moving with his family to Chelsea in London, where he spent most of his school years. He hated school in England, blaming uptight teachers who constantly found fault with his American accent and dialogue, making him stand in the corner for most of his lessons. After his parents divorced when he was 13, Downey moved back to Los Angeles and dropped out of school in the 11th grade. "I did not come from a super, together family," he says. "I was this weird pot-head kid who got off on blowing away frogs with my BB gun."

After a few months of waiting on tables in LA, he won two parts in off-Broadway productions and the $1000-a-week pay-cheque enabled him to indulge in his favourite drugs – heroin and cocaine. His three weeks' work on John Sayles' *Baby, It's You* (1983) was cut down to just one brief glimpse (his friends dubbed the movie 'Maybe It's You') but it wasn't long before the cute young punk was getting noticed. He met his long-time girlfriend Sarah Jessica Parker on the set of Michael Apted's *Firstborn* (1984), he played Bruno Mussolini in the 1985 television biopic *Mussolini: The Untold Story* and had a few scenes in *Weird Science* (1985) as Ian, the high-school jock and tormentor of wimpy heroes Gary (Anthony Michael Hall) and Wyatt (Ian Mitchell-Smith). One scene involved Downey giving them both wedgies and dropping slurpies on them in the mall. Downey then played Keith Gordon's wild sidekick in the Rodney Dangerfield hit *Back to School* (1986) which led to a season presenting the American comedy television show *Saturday Night Live*, performing alongside fellow brat-packer Anthony Michael Hall, although this period is by no means remembered as one of the NBC series' high points.

Downey's first leading role was in *The Pick-Up Artist* (1987) as a compulsive Don Juan who finally falls in love with a museum guide (Molly Ringwald).

Downey stole every scene in his next picture, *Less Than Zero* (1987), an adaptation of Bret Easton Ellis' novel. The director, Marek Kaniewska, had met Downey while studying the lives of self-indulgent rich kids in New York City's night-clubs, as research for the screen adaptation: "There are certain personalities you remember because they have an incredible intensity about them. They're the centre of attraction, they have incredible charm and they're very seductive. They're also incredibly bright and know how to make everyone feel like a million dollars. I met Robert out and about and thought, That's the character for me. And that's the reason I cast him."

Kaniewska describes Downey as an "impulsive actor", although admits this was more than likely down to his drug use at the time: "He's not someone who switches on and off. He's running 24 hours a day and a director just has to tune into that. He can't switch it off himself. He blurs the line between the real and the fantasy. He was incredibly creative. A joy beyond joy as an actor."

Downey maintains he simply had to be high for his role in *Less Than Zero*: "I had to be able to let myself go, to be in a giddy, fuck-it kind of state in order to turn in a good performance. It's the closest I've ever come to leaving a part of myself up there on screen. I consider myself very lucky to have gone through that period with a career and a working respiratory system."

Playing alongside Andrew McCarthy and Jami Gerz, Downey's character allowed the young actor to turn in a powerful performance and led to Rolling Stone magazine declaring him their "Hot Actor of 1988". However, Downey's co-star in *Less Than Zero*, Jami Gerz knew that many of the film's scenes were too close to home: "You had the feeling, 'Is what happens to Julian going to happen to Robert?'"

As soon as he'd completed the film, Downey checked into a 28-day recovery programme in Arizona.

After good reviews for *Less Than Zero*, a series of let-downs followed. He teamed up with Anthony Michael Hall for the unwatchable teen comedy that was *Johnny Be Goode* (1988), a commercial failure which Orion released on video with 'new sexually explicit footage'. Downey then appeared in his father's barely released porno spoof *Rented Lips* (1988) and in Ernest Thompson's self-indulgent directorial debut *1969* (1988). This was followed by two films that failed to get a release in Britain – a romantic lead role opposite Cybill Shepherd in *Chances Are* (1989) and *True Believer* (1989), in which he played James Woods' legal assistant working on a murder case. At this point, Downey still seemed to have tons of street-cred but no real commercial hits to his name. So it came as a surprise when he managed to get equal billing with Mel Gibson for *Air America* (1990) as Billy Covington, a renegade CIA pilot ferrying cargo during the Vietnam War. Downey told producers that it was the first time he'd been sober since he was 12 years old. "He has such energy," said Gibson. "He's a great guy with a great talent. But weird." But despite buddy-buddy black humour, mid-air madness and expensive special effects, in the summer of 1990, audiences decided against Roger Spotiswoode's film, choosing instead to see *Flatliners* and *Ghost*.

After another of his father's farces, *Too Much Sun* (1991), Downey played the slimy producer of a daytime television soap opera in *Soapdish* (1991), a supporting role opposite Kevin Kline and Sally Field. At this point, Downey's relationship with Sarah Jessica Parker was over: "Sarah was maturing. She was reading novels, watching CNN, making friends," says Downey. "At the same time I was pulling 360s in parking lots and disappearing for three days at a time for things which need blood transfusions to recuperate from."

By December 1991, Downey was preparing for a much bigger role. Having shed a stone and studied the best impersonators, he was all set to be *Chaplin*. Certain he was off the drink and drugs, Richard Attenborough was intent on having the role go to Downey rather than an Englishman: "If you bring in a star, someone with other connotations, you start with a disadvantage. [Downey] will be a world figure as an actor within a month of the film opening... He's an extraordinary boy."

Indeed, all his work paid off. Downey was perfect as Chaplin and in 1992, he was nominated for an Oscar. However, despite his acclaimed performance, he still managed to go off the rails again, ending up in rehab in Culver City. A month later, in May 1992, he married the actress Deborah Falconer. They had a son, Indio, in September 1993. At the time, Downey was enjoying more kind reviews for his performances in both Robert Altman's *Short Cuts* (1992) and Ron Underwood's *Heart and Souls* (1993). A year later he was great as the brash tabloid television journalist in Oliver Stone's *Natural Born Killers* (1994) and even started work on an album at his recording studio in Malibu.

Downey turned in a very funny performance as Holly Hunter's gay brother in *Home for the Holidays* (1995), directed by Jodie Foster, and went on to star in Michael Hoffman's *Restoration* (1995), in which he played Charles II's debauched physician Robert Merivel. During shooting, Downey admitted he was spending way to much money ($14,000 a month on clothes alone) and that his cars had been repossessed: "A lot of my stuff goes missing, with the kinds of friends I have – you know, tramps and thieves. I've worked hard for years, but it's all gone. I made *Restoration* for, like, a quarter of what I once earned. Trouble was, I kept spending like I used to. Even now, I am bribing Harvey Weinstein to send me money for Christmas this year. And he did. He sent me a big cheque. I have to get a job soon and I hope it's good. I have nothing."

Things went from bad to worse. In April 1996, Downey's wife, Deborah Falconer left the family home with their son Indio, driven away by his drug-fuelled antics. Three months later, on June 23rd, 1996, Downey was arrested for drink driving and being in possession of heroin, crack cocaine and a .357 Magnum revolver. Then, on July 16th, police were called to a mansion in Malibu. A woman had called 911 after finding a stranger lying unconscious in her young son's bed. When they arrived, officers discovered the man was an Oscar-nominated actor. The 31-year old was charged with trespassing and later apologised to a judge in a Malibu court. He was ordered to check into Exodus Recovery Centre in Marina Del Rey. On July 20th, he escaped from a window, was arrested again and charged with violating his $7000 bail. Nine days later, in a more secure rehab centre, he was placed under 24-hour surveillance.

Despite the bad habits, Downey had still managed to complete filming commitments. The Mike Figgis film *One Night Stand* (1996) was finished the month of his arrest. He played an AIDS patient in a performance Figgis described as "mind-blowing". Downey later teamed up with Sean Penn in his father's film *Hugo Pool* (1997).

Then he was back in jail, this time in Los Angeles, for violating probation after testing positive for drugs. It was March 1998 and Downey was forced to watch that year's Oscars ceremony through steel bars. However, because of the jail's curfew, he didn't get to see *Titanic* pick up the Best Picture award! After 113 days in the slammer, he was out to promote two more films, Neil Jordan's *In Dreams* (1998) and the independent movie *Friends and Lovers* (1998).

August 6, 1999 – back inside again, jailed for another three years for repeatedly breaking the terms of his parole for previous convictions on drugs charges. Still inside, the new millennium got off to a bad start for Downey. In January, he was left battered after a bloody prison brawl. The 5' 8" actor apparently picked a fight with a 6' 2" monster. "When guards entered the cell they found Robert on the floor pleading with the inmate not to hit him any more," confirmed a prison source. Later, a "Free Robert Downey Junior" campaign by fans got him transferred to a treatment centre.

Downey's troubles have undoubtedly caused him to lose out on some parts. Tim Robbins wanted him for *The Cradle Will Rock* (1998), but the project conflicted with the actor's probation restrictions. Nevertheless, according to his people, when he gets out next time, Downey will be committed to staying clean, although the big question on everyone's lips is 'Will he keep his word?' The director James Toback (who gave Downey his first lead role in *The Pick-Up Artist*) recently directed him again in the movie *Two Girls and a Guy* (1998): "Robert is very ambitious. He has a ravenous appetite for money, fame and to do great work. Paradoxically, he's oblivious to making a constructive path to reach that goal. People with one-tenth his talent are more practical in achieving the success they want. Right now, he's in a state of ignorance about himself and his future."

EMILIO ESTEVEZ
Born 12 May 1962
New York City

Hardly surprising that, with a screen legend as a father, Emilio Estevez chose a career in the movie business. However, unlike father Martin Sheen and infamous brother Charlie, he did choose to proudly use his original Spanish family name. Estevez featured in all of the key Brat Pack films – *The Outsiders*, *The Breakfast Club* and *St Elmo's Fire*. He hung out at LA's Hard Rock Cafe, endlessly partied with fellow 80s' teen stars Rob Lowe, Tom Cruise and Sean Penn, got engaged to Demi Moore and became the unofficial leader of the Pack.

Later, Estevez rejected the Brat Pack label saying, "We were just guys being guys. We'd meet to let off a little steam, that was all. We all have to grow up." He also rejects any notion of family influence in his career: "I'm much more ambitious than my father. Everything that's come to me I've earned. I haven't been given stardom. I'm not a pretty boy who was told, 'We're going to make you a star.'"

Nevertheless, it does seem a bit too much of a coincidence that, after avoiding the usual route of television commercials and soap opera roles, at the age of 20 the wannabe actor landed a role opposite his father in a television movie. It was called *In the Custody of Strangers* (1982) and Estevez plays a 16-year-old who goes on a drunken spree and ends up in the slammer for a month after attacking a homosexual.

Estevez got his real break via Tim Hunter's adaptation of SE Hinton's *Tex* (1982) and they both joined more fresh young faces (Patrick Swayze, Ralph Macchio, Rob Lowe, C Thomas Howell and Tom Cruise) in Francis Ford Coppola's film of Hinton's *The Outsiders* (1983). He had a small role in Coppola's film, but caught the eye of a young British film student in Los Angeles. UCLA graduate Alex Cox (who later directed *Sid and Nancy* and *Walker*) was in the process of casting his first feature film *Repo Man* (1984): "Although Emilio only had a small part in *The Outsiders*, he had a little improvisation where they kept the camera rolling at the end of a scene. He goes to the refrigerator and pulls out a bottle of beer and a big chocolate cake. He then sits down and proceeds to drink the beer and eat the entire cake. I thought, 'That's good. I can relate to that. This is a chap I'd like to work with one day.' He understood that you could be in a comedy but still play it straight, which is exactly what I wanted from all the actors in *Repo Man*. He played it straight and made it even funnier. I thought he could've been a great comic actor because he had this deadpan quality, but it really seems that maybe that's also his limitation because when he's tried serious 'acting' in things like *Young Guns*, it becomes really embarrassing. I think he had the potential to be a very interesting actor, but the choices he's made since *Repo Man* were not congruent with that."

But despite putting in a fine performance, Estevez made some unexpected choices. Instead of following it up with more weird and offbeat films, he entered the world of teen movies and endless cheesy locker-room comedies. Cox believes Estevez has never really been sure which way he wanted to go. There was to be a *Repo Man* sequel at one point, with a script called *Waldo's Hawaiian Holiday* which was to feature the original cast members – including Estevez: "Emilio is an odd chap. The last time I ever spoke to him was right before we were about to start work together on the sequel to *Repo Man*, a project Peter McCarthy and I had spent a lot of time on putting together. He called me at the office and went on at length about how much he was looking forward to doing the film and how much he'd wished he'd kept working with me after the original *Repo Man*. He was very enthused and fantasising wildly, coming out with all sorts of statements like, 'If we'd stayed together and made more pictures we could've been like Scorsese and De Niro!' I said, 'Well you know, we could've done more films if you'd read the scripts I'd sent you!' But it's okay, we're going to do this one now and it'll be fun.'

"So Peter got the money in place and the bank loan was all there and then Emilio just walked away. We never found out why. Usually when something like that happens it can be to do with the interference of the actor's agent. But it's not like Emilio has a great career and in this instance, the agent was very annoyed that his client had walked away without any explanation. Then again, who really knows what goes on in the world of actors and their agents. You never really know.

"My own theory is that the principal relationship Emilio has is with his father, and that there's some burden that he carries as a result of being the son of Martin Sheen. I felt that Charlie Sheen seemed to be much more well-adjusted, even though Charlie's supposed to be the bad boy. I felt I could never really count on Emilio because his anger towards his father was going to lead him to betray anyone who he saw in that kind of position. Unfortunately, directors do tend to get put in the fantasy father role by certain actors."

After *Repo Man*, Estevez opted for a part in the John Hughes film *The Breakfast Club* (1985). Estevez played the jock called Andrew. "Emilio was probably closest to his character," says Hughes. "There was a little surfer jock to him. The kid I based him on was a football player, but I got nervous that it was too close, so I changed him to a wrestler."

The Breakfast Club took $46 million in its short theatrical run and became one of the highest grossing releases of 1985. But while Estevez's career was going well, his private life wasn't. His mid-80s girlfriend Carey Salley sued him for child support, claiming he was the father of her two children, Paloma and Taylor. While he denied the claims, his father Martin Sheen provided financial support for Salley. Later, Estevez apologised, saying he'd regretted turning his back on his kids.

Next for Estevez was a role in Joel Schumacher's *St Elmo's Fire*. Estevez, Ally Sheedy and Judd Nelson were the only actors to star in both the definitive Brat Pack movies. During filming on *St Elmo's Fire*, he began dating Demi Moore. The pair got engaged and were supposed to marry on 6 December 1986. The invitations were sent out. Then Demi changed her mind. Later, Estevez began dating make-up artist Sheryl Berkoff. She ended up marrying Rob Lowe.

Four years before *St Elmo's Fire*, on the set of *Tex* in 1982, Estevez befriended the cult author SE Hinton, who hinted that he would be a great Mark Jennings, the protagonist of her novel, *That Was Then, This Is Now*. Estevez secured the film rights to the book and, during breaks in shooting *St Elmo's Fire*, he wrote the draft for what would be the fourth film adaptation of a Hinton novel. *That Was Then, This Is Now* was released in 1986 with Estevez as Mark, the young hustler who lashes out at everyone as he tries to live through adolescence. He is the confused, maybe-gay friend of Craig Sheffer, whose acquiring of a girlfriend is something he can't handle. The film scores points for its cinematography by Juan Ruiz-Anchia, who has skilfully caught the dark drab look of the street. But although there are a few moments when you feel for the characters, the script by Estevez adds nothing new to previous film versions of Hinton's vision of young outsiders rebelling, which is perhaps why cinema audiences weren't interested.

Maximum Overdrive (1986) sees Estevez as an ex-con on probation in North Carolina, working as a cook in a truckstop. What could possibly happen? Well, a giant comet crashes into Earth which turns everything mechanical into killer machines.

Aged 23, Estevez became the youngest Hollywood star to write, direct and star in a movie. *Wisdom* (1986) has Estevez as John Wisdom, a modern-day Robin Hood who helps out farmers and property owners who are having a hard time with the banks during the Reagan years. The film co-starred his then fiancée Demi Moore as his girlfriend who helps him get around the country to hold up banks and destroy mortgage records. The pair become media heroes/national treasures etc… Critics hated it and even Estevez has admitted he has to change channels if his film comes on television.

Nevertheless, Estevez had another taste of success in 1987 with John Badham's *Stakeout*. There's no great chemistry between Estevez and Richard Dreyfuss as two Seattle cops on a surveillance assignment. But the buddy movie had commercial appeal and Estevez could safely smile again at lunches with Hollywood suits. In 1988, he topped the bill of the Brat Pack western, *Young Guns* in the role of Billy the Kid.

After co-starring with daddy in *Nightbreaker* (1988), a television movie about a research neurologist using unwitting soldiers as guinea pigs for their experiments, Estevez scripted and directed himself and brother Charlie in the laughless comedy *Men at Work* (1990). They played two Southern Californian trash collectors who stumble across a body stuffed in a garbage can along their route – a body that just happens to be a local politician mixed up in a toxic waste scandal.

Then came *Young Guns 2: Blaze of Glory* (1990), with Estevez back, cockier than ever, as Billy the Kid. This time he and his gang are pursued across Mexico by a posse led by Pat Garrett (William Peterson).

In the 90s, Estevez went from being a Hollywood star with big teen appeal, to a second-rate actor. He proved he really couldn't handle the macho heroics of a big budget action film, despite top-billing in Geoff Murphy's futuristic flop *Freejack* (1992), and he embarrassed himself in *National Lampoon's Loaded Weapon 1* (1993), *Another Stakeout* (1993) and so on. Many of his own projects simply fell through (including *El Nino* and *Secret Society*, both with dad Martin; *Ask the Dust*, for the French director Daniel Vigne; and *Clear Intent*, based on his own script.) Estevez was also set to play the man responsible for organising the 1969 Woodstock festival in *Young Men With Unlimited Capital* (for Warner Brothers), but according to press reports, the project fell through following rows over billing between Estevez and his co-star Ralph Macchio.

In April 1992, Estevez got hitched to the rock star, Paula Abdul. They married secretly, in Santa Monica, California. On 19th September, they organised a second ceremony (costing $200,000) and invited everyone. Estevez's best man Tom Cruise didn't show up. The couple divorced in 1994.

Even sadder for Estevez was that in an attempt to hang on to any form of commercial success, he signed up to the Disney-produced *Mighty Ducks* franchise. Ten years earlier he was involved in talked-about cutting edge films like *Repo Man* and *The Outsiders*, and a decade on he was entertaining the kids as Gordon Bombay, a smooth operating hockey coach. He'd already made two sequels (*Young Guns 2* and *Another Stakeout*), but failed to learn his lesson, in the end making a total of three *Mighty Ducks* movies: "My kids really wanted me to do them. They're very big on hockey. I didn't want to let them down."

Actually, wasn't it because of the age-old story of a Hollywood studio agreeing to finance the latest actor–director vanity trip in exchange for keeping him or her tied to money-spinning film sequels? When Estevez signed to do *D3: The Mighty Ducks* (1996), Disney forked out 75% of the budget for his directorial effort, *The War at Home* (1996), which he also scripted and starred in. He played a Vietnam vet returning home after the war – which served only to remind the world that Estevez is no more than a bit actor in kid's movies.

ANTHONY MICHAEL HALL
(Michael Anthony Hall)
Born 14 April 1968
Boston, Massachusetts

Anthony Michael Hall was the geek of the Pack. The puny actor's naturally funny performances in *Sixteen Candles* and in *The Breakfast Club* resulted in scores of offers from noted directors (including Stanley Kubrick, who wanted him for the lead role in *Full Metal Jacket* in 1987, reportedly calling Hall's debut the most promising since Jimmy Stewart's.) But after a year of partying with the *Saturday Night Live* gang, directors and casting agents lost interest. Hall was drinking vodka by the quart every day by the time he was 17. This led to much publicised drinking sprees and punch-ups: "A lot of performers get messed up because they think they don't deserve their success, but I was the opposite," he told the *Los Angeles Times* in 1988.

Anthony Michael Hall had to balance school with his career in the movies, making his first film appearance at the age of 14. The Kenny Rogers vehicle *Six Pack* (1982) is a corny comedy about six orphans who are forced to strip cars by a crooked sheriff. They strip one belonging to a stock-car racing driver (Rogers), who then inherits the kids and becomes their father figure. Hall was one of the orphans. Diane Lane was another.

A year later, Hall played Chevy Chase's loyal son Rusty Griswold in the Harold Ramis farce, *National Lampoon's Vacation*. Chase is determined to take his wife and kids to 'Wally World' in California, but on the cross-country ride from Chicago, the family run into one disaster after another. What can go wrong, will go wrong – and Dad's to blame for everything. While mother and daughter let him get on with it, Hall, as Rusty, is more of a help and shares some of the funnier moments with Chase. The film scored financially, but Hall was nowhere to be seen in the sequel *National Lampoon's European Vacation* (1985). Thanks to John Hughes (who scripted but got bounced off *National Lampoon's Vacation*), he'd gone on to better things…

In John Hughes' directorial debut *Sixteen Candles* (1984), Hall is 'the geek'. Even though Hall's character was a secondary one, he was singled out by critics and made a great impression on John Hughes, who offered him a role in his next film, *The Breakfast Club*. "About casting, I was both reckless and careful," says Hughes. "I've only got five people, so there has to be some interesting chemistry between them. It either works or it completely fails. I took Molly and Michael [Anthony Michael Hall's real first name] immediately from *Sixteen Candles*. I'd known him because he played Rusty in *National Lampoon's Vacation*, and I thought he upstaged Chevy Chase, which is kind of hard to do."

The auditions were held in New York City. "I was in the ninth grade," recalls Hall, "and I had the audition at MCA Universal at, like, 57th and Park. I remember walking through the lobby and going, 'Wow! This is really cool!' We were literally at the end of *Sixteen Candles* when John approached Molly and me, separately, and told us about this other project, and I was like, 'I don't have to read for this? I'm in!'"

"Michael came in his Catholic school uniform: the loose tie, khaki pants, and big Nike tennis shoes," recalls Hughes. "Michael kept his braces on for this part. People may say, 'So what?' But when you're that age and you've been wearing those damn braces for four years, to say you're going to wear them for another six months because this character should have braces is pretty amazing. Molly and Michael were 16 and 15, so we only had four hours a day with them [because of child labour laws]. We'd shoot them out early, so by the end of the day Ally was reading with stand-ins. After about three weeks, Molly asked me if she was ever going to get to do a scene with anybody."

But apart from the time constraints for filming, Hall was mostly pissed off about his age because he couldn't go out partying with co-stars Judd Nelson and Emilio Estevez: "They could go out and have a beer. I had to retreat to the room and finish my homework. I was just trying to figure out when puberty would end," he says. Hall does, however, fondly remember his time on set: "To this day, what sticks in my mind is John, behind the camera, either laughing or crying. He was so great to all of us, particularly Molly and me. He made me feel like family. He made all of us feel like that."

One of Hall's key scenes was the pot-smoking scene. Hughes shot 20 minutes of footage, all completely ad-libbed: "It would have been a freakin' miniseries if they'd given us real weed," laughs Hall. "At the time, I was a huge Richard Pryor fan. 'Chicks cannot hold their smoke' – that scene where we're all getting high – was Richard Pryor. We were just laughing our asses off in rehearsal."

Near the end of filming, Ringwald and Hall dated for a while: "Puppy love stuff," explains Hall. "It was a surprise to me because throughout *Sixteen Candles* and into *The Breakfast Club* there was a little tension between us. I didn't know how to approach her. I had seen *Tempest*, and I just remember thinking she was hot. So I kept a healthy distance from her on *Sixteen Candles*, but I really had a crush on her the whole time. And then, three-quarters of the way through *The Breakfast Club*, Molly just initiated it. I'm 15, making movies and Molly Ringwald is interested in me. I'm just going, 'This is too good!' She was very womanly."

"They were sort of wonderful together," recalls Ally Sheedy. "*Sixteen Candles* had opened right at the end of shooting, and suddenly Michael had girls chasing him down the street. It was crazy! I thought Molly was great for him then because she was savvy about fame and understood it."

The romance between Hall and Ringwald, however, proved to be very short-lived.

But the film was a big hit and brought fame (and more teen roles) to Hall. Hughes offered him the lead role in his next film, the comedy/sci-fi spoof, *Weird Science* (1985) about two frustrated teens who use their home computer and a Barbie doll to create the perfect woman.

After *The Breakfast Club*, everyone agreed Hughes' *Weird Science* was a big disappointment. Nevertheless, the idea and characters were turned into a successful weekly American television series. As for Hall, his working relationship with John Hughes ended. He turned down roles in *Pretty in Pink* and *Ferris Bueller's Day Off* to avoid being typecast. Hall wanted to grow up (as did John Hughes) and set about transforming his image. After a year on the NBC show *Saturday Night Live*, Hall appeared in Richard Tuggle's *Out of Bounds* (1986), a thriller devoid of any suspense. A very confused-looking Hall muddles his way through as an Iowa farm boy who arrives in LA, picks up the wrong bag at the airport and finds he's become the city's most wanted criminal. The bag is full of heroin which really belongs to murderous drug dealers. Hall transforms himself into a typical LA street kid with cred so he can evade both the LAPD and the gangsters.

Worse was to come. Hall was hired by Stanley Kubrick to star in his contribution to the Vietnam genre, *Full Metal Jacket,* but he got fired after repeatedly complaining about Kubrick's time-consuming and perfectionist directing style. Hall was replaced by Mathew Modine. Who knows what might have been if Hall had just kept his mouth shut…

Instead, the unwatchable *Johnny Be Goode* was a return to teen comedy for Hall, who plays Johnny Walker, a high-school football star at the top of every major college team's recruitment list. They'll do anything to get him and he'll take anything that's on offer. Maybe someone should have mentioned it was a bit much to ask anyone to take the gangly Anthony Michael Hall at all seriously as 'the hottest high-school quarterback in the nation'.

By 1990, however, Hall looked as if he'd being working out at the gym. Well-built and more mature-looking, the former geek began to tackle adult roles. "I've had to hustle and take things you don't necessarily want to be in," he said. He played Winona Ryder's highly unlikeable psycho boyfriend in *Edward Scissorhands* and appeared with Will Smith in *Six Degrees of Separation*. Hall then turned director with *Hail Caesar,* which featured cameos from his old brat pack pals Judd Nelson and Robert Downey Jr.

However, by the late 90s, Hall was back to playing geeks. Obviously not high-schoolers but adult wimps. He played Microsoft boss Bill Gates in the made-for-television movie *Pirates of Silicon Valley*.

ROB LOWE
Robert Hepler Lowe
Born 17 March 1964
Charlottesville, Virginia

Rob Lowe was the Leonardo DiCaprio of his time and the essence of a true Brat Packer. This pretty boy partied with best buddies Emilio Estevez and Judd Nelson and dated a string of famous women, from actresses Melissa Gilbert ("I was a Brat Pack wife," she claims) and Nastassja Kinski to Grace Jones, Brooke Shields and Princess Stephanie of Monaco: "If I haven't been with 'em, I know 'em, or I've been engaged to 'em. I looked at my calendar and said, 'Shit, it's a few weeks into the new year and I haven't been engaged to anyone yet. I'd better get to work.'"

But despite his cute looks, it would have perhaps been better for him if he wasn't so attractive. Because for all the varying roles (comedy, drama and mystery), Lowe's boyishness always somehow got in the way and he never got beyond being seen as a lightweight actor. It's the same story again. Like Robert Downey Jr, his private life became far more interesting than his film work and he made a name for himself mainly through gossip and scandal. Remember that naughty video?

The son of a lawyer, Robert Helper Lowe grew up in Dayton, Ohio. He spent much of his youth on stage and in television commercials. At 12, he moved with his family to Malibu, where he went to school with Emilio Estevez and Charlie Sheen. They began making their own home videos (a talent which later caused Lowe major embarrassment) and later entered the LA acting scene. Lowe got a couple of Coca-Cola commercials and landed a part in a television sitcom called *A New Kind of Family* in 1979.

After a few more television specials, he made his big-screen debut in Francis Ford Coppola's *The Outsiders* as Soda Pop, a gas attendant and the older brother to troubled Pony Boy (C. Thomas Howell). Then, Lowe was nominated for a Golden Globe award for his role in the television movie *Thursday's Child* (1983), in which he played a 17-year-old boy in search of a transplant donor for his chronically diseased heart.

Lowe got star billing in his next film, *Class* (1983), a coming-of-age movie full of 80s excess. "Rob sort of came with the package," recalls *Class* director Lewis John Carlino. "He was perfect for the role. I had seen him in *The Outsiders* and liked his look and what little work he had to do in that film. I was looking for someone appealing, who in a naïve, charming, way represented the privileged class and all the attitudes that come with it. The trick was to find someone who really was not self-conscious of what he represented. His lack of guile, openness and sweetness was what I was after. Rob, at the time, was all of these things, both in the role and his persona. We became good friends and it was a delight to work with him. Unfortunately, Rob had a major glitch in his career with that video debacle, but I find, like Andrew McCarthy, after they both got past the silly stage, each has done some interesting work. I think they both continue to mature and I'm pleased to see them being given some very interesting roles."

After *Class* came *The Hotel New Hampshire* (1984), Tony Richardson's stylish adaptation of John Irving's 1981 novel. Not surprisingly, Lowe was a good-looking bad boy type who had his way with Jodie Foster and Nastassja Kinski.

In *Oxford Blues*, Lowe is Nicky D'Angelo, a cocky Las Vegas car valet who wangles his way on to the entry list for Oxford University in order to meet his dream woman. Lowe put in a more charismatic performance in *St Elmo's Fire* as Billy Hixx, the immature, sax-playing bit of rough who can't hold down a job.

In *Youngblood*, he and Patrick Swayze starred as ice-hockey players, in a very lame, soapy vehicle for Lowe. The film was a complete flop. *About Last Night*, the adaptation of David Mamet's *Sexual Perversity in Chicago*, teamed Lowe with Demi Moore. In his next film, *Square Dance* (1987), he took a huge pay cut and accepted fourth billing to appear as a young mentally handicapped Texan boy. His performance won him another Golden Globe nomination and praise from some critics: "I don't think Lowe gets enough credit. He has a real talent. He could be like Alain Delon, playing high-quality villains – interesting, complex people. I could see him playing Ted Bundy," wrote New York critic Andrew Sarris. But it was down to earth with a bump when Lowe's next film, the courtroom comedy, *Illegally Yours* (1988) bombed. Lowe was totally miscast as a silly college dropout on jury duty, who finds the defendant is a girl he's had a crush on since first grade.

In Bob Swaim's *Masquerade* (1988), Lowe is a handsome, fortune-hunting gigolo preying on rich girl Kim Cattrall. The character seemed too much of a stretch for him and the clumsy dialogue didn't help.

1988 was not a good year for Lowe. His on-and-off girlfriend for six years, Melissa Gilbert (of *Little House on the Prairie*) decided finally to break up with him for good. However, the first Lowe heard of it was when she called up a radio station to broadcast the news she was to marry the actor-producer-director Bo Brinkman. Then, on 17th July, Lowe was in Atlanta as a celebrity supporter of the Democrat party in the US Presidential election campaign. At rallies, he came across as an intelligent, concerned young American. But later that evening, his actions would lead to the biggest Hollywood sex scandal in years.

At a party, Lowe got chatting with 16-year-old Lena Jan Parsons and her friend, 22-year-old Tara Siebert. They all retired to Lowe's hotel room, where he set up a video camera to tape the sex sessions. While Lowe was in the bathroom, the two girls stole money from his wallet and the video cassette. Jan's mother found the tape a month later and court proceedings began in 1989 after a $35,000 out-of-court settlement was rejected. A civil suit filed against Lowe claimed he "used his celebrity status as an inducement to females to engage in sexual intercourse, sodomy and multiple-part sexual activity for his immediate gratification and for the purpose of making pornographic films of these activities".

Later, copies of the tape began to circulate and ended up on the networked television series *A Current Affair,* as well as the X-rated cable show *Midnight Blue.* No charges were actually brought against the actor, but by then it was too late. The whole world had seen or heard about his sexual encounter with a 16-year-old girl. "There's no way you can know how embarrassing it was," he told *People* magazine in 1990. Copies of the home video fetched $250 on the black market, with US chat show host Arsenio Hall joking: "At last, Rob Lowe has made a film everyone wants to see!"

Lowe quit drinking and joined a clinic to help him cope with his above-average sexual appetite. For a while, it seemed nobody wanted to know him and he was reduced to supporting roles on stage in New York. However, two years after the incident in Atlanta, Lowe played a seductive charmer in the psychological thriller *Bad Influence* (1990). His bad boy image helped enormously with the publicity for a film which ironically revolved around sexually compromising video tapes!

In 1991, Lowe married Emilio Estevez's ex-girlfriend, the make-up artist Sheryl Berkoff. Up until that point, Estevez and Lowe had been best pals, but Emilio wasn't happy: "There's an unwritten rule between guys who are friends – you don't go out with your buddy's ex-girlfriend. And you certainly don't marry her."

As Lowe began to concentrate on his family (the couple soon had two sons, Matthew and John), Hollywood executives started to call him again. He was cast by Lorne Michaels in 1992's *Wayne's World,* playing the greedy television executive Benjamin Oliver. It was a supporting role in a film based on two *Saturday Night Live* characters, Wayne and Garth (the then-unknown comics Mike Myers and Dana Carvey). But the film was a hit and grossed $132 million on its first US release, Lowe's most successful to date.

Since working his way back into the big league, Lowe has appeared in the much-hyped Stephen King television mini-series *The Stand* (1993), the dark western *Frank and Jesse* (1994), in which he played Jesse James opposite Bill Paxton as Frank, and he was also hired by Lorne Michaels again for *Tommy Boy* (1995), a comedy starring the late Chris Farley. He lost out to Colin Firth for the role of Darcy in BBC television's adaptation of *Pride and Prejudice*, but landed a cameo in *Mulholland Falls* (1996). He's also appeared as a Christian Rights Activist in *Contact* (1997) with Jodie Foster and in the recent Mike Myers vehicle *Austin Powers II: The Spy Who Shagged Me* (1999), which was a big hit at the box office.

Rob Lowe is back on track. He will probably never achieve the fame and adulation he received (mainly from teenage girls) again in his career, but he has now appeared in a few extra hits, despite having been labelled as 'unemployable' by many, and his new television comedy series *West Wing* was hailed as one of the best of 1999 by American television critics. Based in a fictional White House, it was Lowe's first network television series: "This is the acting role I've been waiting for all my life," he admits. "When I read scripts for the show, I felt like it had been written for me. I really believed I was the only guy who could do it and I don't know if that's happened to me before."

Nevertheless, in terms of Brat Pack history, Rob Lowe's indiscretion at the 1988 Democratic convention will never be forgotten and can be seen as one of the key events which caused the destruction of that group of self-promoting stars. As the 1980s drew to a close, party-mad actors like Lowe were coming to be resented by the tabloids, rather than celebrated.

RALPH MACCHIO
Born 4 November 1962
Long Island, New York

Like Matthew Broderick, Ralph Macchio's deceptively young looks have kept him in work for much of his career. He earned fame and fortune as Daniel in the series of *Karate Kid* films, but disappeared from the limelight when he failed to escape the domain of teenage roles.

Macchio comes from a family that owns a large trucking company in New York. He began singing and dancing in amateur musical productions when he was still in high school and by the time he was 16, he started landing parts in television commercials. He auditioned for the film director Robert Downey, who gave him a part in his uneven comedy *Up the Academy* (1980), and then spent two years as Jeremy Andretti on the US television series *Eight is Enough*.

Three years after his film debut for Downey, Macchio landed a part in Francis Ford Coppola's *The Outsiders* (1983), the film that marked the birth of the Brat Pack. Macchio gives a strong, intelligent performance as Johnny, a greaser who ends up killing a boy in order to save his friend. Truly impressive as the doomed friend, Macchio seemed set for a promising future.

Obviously desperate to match the glory days of *Rocky*, the director John G Avildsen decided to make it again. Even the musical score is written by the man who created the theme for Rocky, Bill Conti, and there's also a song on the soundtrack called *Moment of Truth* by Survivor, the group that sang *Eye of the Tiger*. But this time all of the action takes place in the world of karate, rather then boxing.

"My films are about people who have dreams, because I'm prone to fairy-tales," remarked Avildsen. His formula was a success – the film grossed more than $100 million at the American box office and it spawned two sequels, which similarly pulled in the crowds.

A few more teen roles followed: Arthur Hill's very disappointing high-school black comedy *Teachers* (1984), an over-sentimental television movie called *The Three Wishes of Billy Grier* (1984) about a boy dying from a rare ageing illness, and *Crossroads*

(1986), a film by Walter Hill about a classical guitar student called Eugene (Macchio) who meets crotchety old bluesman Willie Brown (Joe Seneca), a one-time playing companion of the legendary Robert Johnson, in a New York hospital. "Where I come from, you don't play no harp, you don't get no pussy," he says. Not quite as gracious as old Mr Miyagi, this old geezer drags Eugene across the Mississippi Delta country in order to teach him Johnson's alleged 'unknown 30th song'.

Karate Kid II was in 1986, this time set in the Far East, and again directed by John G Avildsen. The film begins exactly where the original left off, with Daniel winning a karate contest against the local bullies. On hearing his father is seriously ill, mentor Miyagi heads for his native Okinawa and takes Macchio with him. Miyagi meets his old enemy, another ageing karate expert called Sato, whose nephew happens to take a disliking to Macchio.

The sequel was certainly inferior and failed to allow the character of Daniel to mature beyond the age of 17. By this point Macchio was really 24 and decided to take time out from film roles to concentrate on theatre work. Later in 1986, he appeared opposite Robert DeNiro on Broadway in *Cuba and his Teddy Bears*, for which he received some great reviews.

In *Distant Thunder* (1988), Vietnam veteran John Lithgow leaves his Washington retreat to see the son (Macchio) he hasn't seen in 15 years. But when they return to the wild rain forests, violence breaks out and both must decide if they are truly family or just strangers with the same name. Rick Rosenthal's film is too sentimental and clichéd, but nowhere near as bad as…

…the final film in John G Avildsen's series, *Karate Kid III* (1989). A boring, dismal affair with a story we've seen twice already. It's yet another 'all-action martial arts adventure', with Daniel returning to fight his most difficult battle, this time against a ruthless man out to destroy not only him but Mr Miyagi as well! The only remarkable thing about the film was that Ralph Macchio still looked young enough to play a 17-year-old. But, even three years later, he was playing a college boy in Jonathan Lynn's *My Cousin Vinny*, who enlists the help of his inexperienced lawyer cousin, Joe Pesci.

For the rest of the 90s, Macchio was resigned to supporting roles, usually in very low-budget films, most of which failed to get distribution. One of the better known films was *Naked in New York* (1994), in which he appeared as young writer Eric Stolz's best friend, Chris. In 1995, he guested in an episode of the television sci-fi series *The Outer Limits*, but by 1996 he was in touring theatrical productions such as the musical *How to Succeed in Business Without Really Trying*, which ended up playing in 39 US cities.

The main problem for Ralph Macchio is that the success of *Karate Kid* and the other teen pictures he appeared in marginalised him in that sort of role. It could only last for so long. In the 90s, he was in his thirties, and a married man with kids of his own can't carry on playing a 17-year-old forever. Now soon to be in his forties, Macchio faces an uncertain future, wondering how to forge some sort of significant alternative screen identity for himself.

ANDREW McCARTHY
Born 29 November 1962
Westfield, New Jersey

Andrew McCarthy was the Mr Nice of the 1980s, the sensitive, caring, sensible member of the Brat Pack. The characters he played always seemed a touch more intellectual and deeper than those played by Lowe, Estevez and Nelson.

Born in New Jersey, he attended prep school before moving to New York to study acting at the city's University. It wasn't long before he was acting at the Circle in the Square Theatre as well as other productions. McCarthy's feature-film debut came in the coming-of-age movie *Class* (1983). The film's director, Lewis John Carlino, met McCarthy at an open casting call in New York: "Andy had done some theatre work in and around New York and had some stage skills. I tested him and the production team agreed he had a strange off-beat quality that worked in the role. As the character he was the total obverse of Rob, always playing it close to his chest, somewhat mistrustful, and introverted, with the wounded look in his eyes and in his smile; a character who was never really comfortable in the world. For me, they played well against each other. I haven't looked at the film for a long time, but I think it was part of that genre of Brat Pack films. I had intended to make *Class* a more serious piece in a Salinger-esque sense, but it came out pretty much a popcorn summer movie. I had sought to make something of a little more substance, but so much for might-have-been."

Nevertheless, Carlino's film was a success at the box office. But it was in *St Elmo's Fire* that McCarthy's career began to take off with a performance as the shy college graduate Kevin.

St Elmo's Fire ensured his Brat Pack status, although McCarthy describes the label as "pejorative" and maintains he kept himself to himself on set and stayed away from the wild parties. "Only in hindsight was I aware that it was a big deal," he explains. "I don't think I've seen any of those people since we finished *St Elmo's Fire*. And I've never met Anthony Michael Hall."

A starring role alongside Kevin Dillon and Mary Stuart Masterson in the Catholic boys' school comedy *Heaven Help Us* (1985) was followed up with another shy boy role in Howard Deutch's *Pretty in Pink* (1986) – this time as a rich kid courting poor girl Molly Ringwald.

Next, McCarthy played a window-dresser who falls for a department store dummy (Kim Cattrall) in the plastic-wrapped 80s fantasy *Mannequin* (1987). If it had not been such an unexpected commercial hit, McCarthy's career could have ended here.

Instead, he landed a role in Marek Kanievska's adaptation of Bret Easton Ellis' novel, *Less Than Zero* (1987), as stressed-out Clay (another performance of pure panic), who returns from college for the Christmas break to find his old friends have become junkies and no-hopers. But by this time, the Brat Pack craze was already dying down – and McCarthy's career suffered as a result.

Waiting for the Moon (1987), in which McCarthy played an American in Europe, wasn't given a full theatrical release, while *Fresh Horses* (1988) simply went through the *Pretty In Pink* motions by having McCarthy as a college boy who falls for Molly Ringwald (again). And McCarthy looked decidedly out for the count by 1988, when he joined Matt Dillon as yet another teen involved in a dull romance (this time with a rich farm girl) in Kansas.

Nevertheless, McCarthy got to work with the acclaimed French director Claude Chabrol in his next two films – *Clichy Days* (1989) and *Docteur M* (1990). He did, however, find it increasingly hard to get decent film roles in the 90s. He stayed with comedy for Ted Kotcheff's *Weekend at Bernies* (1989), in which he and Jonathan Silverman played two young hustlers far down the corporate ladder. But both were upstaged by the corpse, Bernie (Terry Kiser again), in the sequel four years later. McCarthy then had a small role in Lee Tamahori's *Mullholland Falls* (1996) and most recently he's appeared as Kurt Bishop in the Rutger Hauer action movie *New World Disorder* (1999) and in his brother Justin McCarthy's directorial debut *Jump* (1999). McCarthy's also gone back to the stage, with a role in the off-Broadway production of *Psychopathia Sexualis*.

DEMI MOORE
(Demetria Guynes)
Born 11 November 1962
Roswell, New Mexico

Only two Brat Packers seemed to emerge from the eighties even more successful than before. Tom Cruise is one; the other is Demi Moore. Like Cruise, Moore has always been intensely ambitious. She's always wanted real power in Hollywood and, like her male counterpart, she's succeeded.

Moore was born in 1962 in Roswell, New Mexico (yep, where the aliens are kept). She had an unhappy childhood; her father left before she was born, while her stepfather was in and out of work and spent more time gambling than he did with his daughter. The family moved around at least 40 times until the drinking and arguing got too much for Moore's father, who finally committed suicide. Furthermore, the young Demetria had one more problem she had to overcome before she could even begin to think about fulfilling her ambitions. She had been born severely cross-eyed and she knew she'd have to get it put right. Eventually, after two operations, the condition was fixed.

Moore quit school when she was 16, went to LA and got work as a pin-up girl, appearing nude in *Oui*. At 18, she married the rock musician Freddy Moore, 12 years her senior. The couple moved into their new home next door to Nastassja Kinski. They became good friends and Demi Moore decided she wanted to be an actress. She soon landed a regular role on the American daytime soap opera *General Hospital*. She was popular with the series' faithful audience and stayed on the show for three years (1981–1983).

During her time on *General Hospital*, Moore managed to take a few roles in films which gave her little chance to shine – *Choices* (1981) and *Young Doctors in Love* (1982). In 1984 came her first lead role, that of a wannabe singer, performing in seedy nightclubs, who becomes the object of a young photographer's devotion in *No Small Affair*. Moore was cast in the film by Craig Baumgarten: "I knew from the very, very beginning Demi was going to be a movie star. I knew it when I saw the dailies on *No Small Affair*. She can rip your heart out, make you care. That's a rare quality and part of what makes a star. When she was in pain, you just wanted to make her feel better."

No Small Affair wasn't much to write home about, but Moore managed to look sexy and caught the eye of Joel Schumacher, who was about to begin casting his film *St Elmo's Fire*. Moore became an official Brat Packer and played Jules, the glamorous, drug-taking high-flyer who goes from one crisis to another, ending up a suicidal wreck.

Unfortunately, the party lifestyle and coke-sniffing weren't confined to Moore's character in the film. She turned up high on set one day and was fired on the spot. She sought treatment and returned after a week, although she was forced to sign a new contract stipulating she would stop all drug and alcohol abuse, which can't have been easy, given that she was playing a coke addict.

While filming *St Elmo's Fire*, Moore began dating Emilio Estevez. They got engaged and spent three years together. They also starred together in Estevez's writing and directorial debut *Wisdom* (1986). In the same year, Moore starred with Rob Lowe in *About Last Night*. She plays all the romantic notes in a film which has her less shallow and stupid than she was in *St Elmo's Fire*. The film lacks much of Mamet's acerbic wit, although both Moore and Lowe are likeable in a story about the biggest hang-up of youth – what is real love and will it hurt me? The following year, Moore was called on to save the planet when she starred in the apocalyptic thriller *The Seventh Sign.*

Moore began the 90s by escaping the youth scene. She ditched Emilio Estevez, cancelling their wedding after the invitations had already been sent out, and accused him of not being able to offer her any security. She then starred in *Ghost* (1990), the silly and sentimental thriller that became the biggest box-office hit of the 90s (perhaps because of its fundamentalist view of heaven and hell). Jerry Zucker's film had Moore as Molly, the wife of murdered stockbroker Patrick Swayze, who returns as a ghost to protect her and hunt down his killers.

Having married Bruce Willis (they called a priest at midnight in Las Vegas after watching a boxing match there), Moore starred with him in her own production *Mortal Thoughts* (1991), and played the female lead in Dan Aykroyd's disappointing directorial debut, *Nothing But Trouble* (1991), which turned out to be exactly that. She also sought to capitalise on her successes by making sure she remained in the glare of the media. Her skill for publicity stunts led to her appearance – nude and seven months pregnant with her second child – on the cover of an issue of *Vanity Fair* in 1991, and again in 1992, when this time she posed nude wearing body paint that resembled a man's suit.

Such stunts caused controversy, but also helped her win the much-coveted female leads in *A Few Good Men* (1992) and *Indecent Proposal* (1993). As the 90s progressed, Moore's icy public persona ensured she was continually offered stronger, harder roles. Known as one of Hollywood's most awkward, she asked for a $5 million pay cheque for *Disclosure* (1994). Then on-set she demanded a double-size trailer, with a lawn and a forest of fig trees outside – and she got her way. The film, a tale of sexual harassment in the work place, features Moore as a predatory female executive who sets her sights on seducing her ex-love and office subordinate, Michael Douglas.

On hearing that Douglas received $12 million for *Disclosure*, Moore then demanded $12.5 million for her next project, *Striptease* (1996), in which she bared all again, as the girl who gets her kit off to keep custody of her child. Despite Moore stripping on the American *Late Show* with David Letterman to promote *Striptease*, it seemed audiences were beginning to lose interest in such staged controversy and the film was a failure at the box office, as was *The Scarlet Letter*.

The recent *GI Jane* was more successful, and Moore also became the highest paid actor in a Woody Allen film in 1997 (she got $450,000 for her role in *Deconstructing Harry*). In 1998 she was back on the front pages of the tabloids again with the announcement that her marriage of 11 years to Bruce Willis was to end. No reasons were given, although reporters were alleging she'd had an affair with Leonardo DiCaprio and printed pictures of him leaving her mansion the morning after they'd spent a romantic day out in Los Angeles.

Demi Moore is still looking to repeat the success of her films of the early 90s, where she had warmer, softer roles, which audiences seemed to prefer. Nevertheless, at the moment she still seems to command the huge fees she desires so much, although it remains to be seen how much longer she can justify $12.5 million without filling theatres.

MOLLY RINGWALD
Born 18 February 1968
Roseville, California

Molly Ringwald was the red-haired young movie star who had teens queuing at the cinema and attracted a huge following of groupies (Ringlets), who would dye their hair orange, smear on the lipstick and parade around in Molly-style punk gear. More 'normal' than Madonna, Ringwald was still seen as hip, even though she was a typical white American teen. She made the cover of *Time* magazine in 1986 and was labelled the 'Princess of the Brat Pack', although she wasn't really a part of the Brat Pack social scene; like her one-time boyfriend Anthony Michael Hall, she was six years younger than the rest of the gang. Ringwald was the fresh young face of the 80s, although after her rapid rise to stardom, it took even less time for her to all but disappear.

Ringwald began her career when she was just three years old, singing with her father's Fulton Street Jazz Band at state fairs and concerts. She recorded her first album *I Wanna Be Loved By You*, at six, which was released in 1974. Her first break into acting was as Kate in a West Coast production of *Annie*, a role she landed after being spotted on TVs *The New Mickey Mouse Show*. Ringwald then joined the American television series *The Facts of Life* in 1979, playing the part of Molly. She left a year later to star in her first feature film *Tempest* (1982), directed by Paul Mazursky, who also auditioned her for the role: "I came in," says Ringwald, "and Paul told me he was going to throw a penny at me for every dumb thing I said. Whatever I said, plink, he just kept tossing them. Pretty soon he was throwing nickels and quarters and dollars, and I just kept talking. When the interview was over, I reached down and gathered up all the money and put it in my pocket. He asked if he could have his money back, and I said no."

Ringwald's performance in *Tempest* led to a Golden Globe award and inspired the writer-director John Hughes to write *Sixteen Candles* for her: 'I was sent this picture of Molly in which she looked like a female version of Huck Finn. She was kind of boyish and interesting – not a beauty – but she had a real honest, innocent look. I stuck her picture up in my office and as I was writing I couldn't stop staring at her,' explains Hughes. Ringwald was only 15 years old when she first met Hughes, at a hotel in Los Angeles: 'He was not at all like other directors I'd met,' she recalls. 'He had really spiky hair, and glasses and cool tennis shoes.' *Sixteen Candles* was the first in the Hughes–Ringwald trilogy. As well as Ringwald, *Sixteen*

Candles includes Anthony Michael Hall and John and Joan Cusack in the teen ensemble. Interestingly, Jim Carrey failed the audition for the role of Ted the Geek (Hall).

The Breakfast Club, the second Hughes-Ringwald movie, centres on a cross-section of high-school kids, whose lives revolve around detention and problems of adolescence.

Ringwald and Hughes were very close, which led to her being seen by the other actors as teacher's pet. However, according to Judd Nelson, that helped in creating the on-screen sexual tension between Claire and John: "Molly was Hughes's girl, and I would push it, you know? What Claire represented was what Bender wanted to fuck metaphorically – not her. Any time John took Molly aside, coddled her, babied her, I loved it. It helped me."

By the end of filming *The Breakfast Club*, Ringwald had begun dating Anthony Michael Hall. However, the romance was short-lived: 'We were like oil and water,' says Ringwald.

The third Hughes–Ringwald film, *Pretty in Pink* (1986) directed by Howard Deutch, focused even further on the class divide between yuppie parents and white trash parents of the 80s and how the children of both had to cope with the superficiality of that decade.

John Hughes undoubtedly made Molly Ringwald a household name. But then things started to go wrong. She turned down the Laura Dern role in the surprise cult hit of the 80s, *Blue Velvet,* (1986) and instead opted to play a museum tour guide opposite Robert Downey Jr's 'artist' in James Toback's awful *The Pick-Up Artist* (1987). Warren Beatty produced it and cast Ringwald after being struck by her "level of intelligence and spontaneity, the lack of affectation in her acting. And obviously her good looks." But subsequently Beatty took his name off the film. Ringwald's career continued to dive with Jean-Luc Godard's mad rendition of Shakespeare's *King Lear*. The film was enigmatic and confusing, with cameos from Woody Allen and Norman Mailer. Ringwald looks great, but this was never going to be a mainstream hit.

In John G Avilsen's *For Keeps* (1988) there's a new slant on the Brat Pack comedy drama, with Ringwald as Darcy, a pregnant teenager, staying the same age but accepting adult responsibilities. She gets pregnant by dream boyfriend Stan (Randall Batinkoff) and has to spend her final year at school waddling around listening to the bitchiness of her fellow classmates. Unlike previous Ringwald characters, she refuses to accept help from her parents and stays put in their hellish apartment.

Immediately following this moderately successful outing came the *Pretty in Pink* rip-off *Fresh Horses* (1988), which was slated by the critics and won Ringwald some terrible publicity for her behaviour on set. To cap it all, the last film she appeared in the eighties, *Loser Takes All* aka *Strike it Rich* (1989) failed to get a release.

After turning down the Demi Moore role in *Ghost* (1990), Ringwald quit Hollywood, moved to France, got married, learned to speak French fluently and even appeared in the French film *Enfants de Salaud*.

When she did finally return to Hollywood, Ringwald landed a role in an ABC television series *Townies*, but no-one switched on and the sitcom was cancelled halfway through its first season. Then, in 1999, the successful screenwriter Kevin Williamson (*Scream / I Know What You Did Last Summer*) gave her a part in his directorial debut, *Teaching Mrs Tingle* (as a substitute teacher). But the spate of high-school shootings at the time resulted in audiences' understandable lack of interest in a film about kids getting their own back on a teacher.

Still in her early thirties, Ringwald is one of the many former Brat Packers who face the new millennium wondering how to pick up the threads of an uneven Hollywood career.

JUDD NELSON
Born 28 November 1959
Portland, Maine

Like Emilio Estevez and Ally Sheedy, Judd Nelson appeared in the two key Brat Pack films – *The Breakfast Club* and *St Elmo's Fire*. Like his rebellious character in the former, Nelson was just as wild in real life. In the 80s, he partied with the coolest kids in Hollywood, he rode a Harley and dated a string of actresses, including Shannen Doherty.

His father was a lawyer, his mother a Congresswoman for the family's home state of Maine. They sent Nelson to the renowned Haverford College, where he studied philosophy. After graduating he studied at New York's Stella Adler Conservatory, appearing in two Pushkin plays as well as a few New York University student films. His feature film debut came in the teen high-school comedy *Making the Grade* (1984), which he followed up with a lead role opposite Kevin Costner in *Fandango* (1985), a rites of passage picture about five college buddies who go on one last fling – an epic adventure across America – before flying to Vietnam to face up to their futures.

In *The Breakfast Club*, a domineering Nelson led the group on Saturday detention and seemed to have the assured confidence lacking in other teen stars of his generation. As John Bender, he was the antagonist – a trouble-making rebel with attitude. Nelson was the last character to be cast in Hughes' film. Originally, John Cusack had been cast when the film was to have been produced by the A&M studio, but when Universal took over John Hughes found himself then having to choose between Nelson, Cusack and Nicolas Cage for the part of Bender. Casting director Jackie Burch helped him decide: "It was touchy because John Hughes was against Judd Nelson at the very end. I just said to him, 'I'm telling you right now, go with Judd Nelson. It's the way this movie should be.'" So Hughes agreed to one final read through with Nelson and Cusack.

"There were 20 people in the room," recalls Nelson. "It was like a performance. I was listening to the Sex Pistols on my Walkman, loud, and I just kicked the headset off, didn't turn the sound off, and just started. Loud. You know, just obnoxious."

"He came in character," says Anthony Michael Hall. "Dickies pants rolled up into his boots, untied laces, the long overcoat, the glove. Judd just came in pissed off. We all kind of looked at each other and said, 'Okay. That's him.'"

Ally Sheedy agrees: "The first time I saw Judd I completely fell in love with him. He was outside the window at the studio with a tennis ball, and he was slamming it against the wall. He just looked like a wild animal. I turned around to John and said, 'Who is that?'"

Hughes agreed Cusack "just didn't look threatening enough" and hired Nelson. Jackie Burch then had to break the bad news to Cusack: "When I said, 'We're going to pay for your airline ticket back,' he said, 'Big deal.' He was so angry."

During the three weeks of rehearsal, Nelson hung out with the real school kids at Glenbrook North, John Hughes' old high-school in Northbrook: "I went to this Laundromat in character, just looking at the ladies. Someone called the cops. I said, 'Look, I'm just an actor.' They're like, 'Sure you are, buddy.'" Then filming began (in sequence): "So many times, we would shoot until we heard this tick, tick, tick," recalls Nelson. "The film magazine had run out on the camera. I think we made our script supervisor retire. First he took notes. Then he used a tape recorder. Then he was, like, gone."

Early in the shoot it became clear that Nelson and Hughes simply weren't getting on. "Judd could be arrogant as anything, but he was really smart, really quick-witted. And he was an uncanny observer. He knew where your Achilles' heels were," recalls the film's publicist Fredell Pogodin. Molly Ringwald believes she was to blame for friction between Nelson and Hughes: "Judd was getting a little bit in character, trying to get under my skin, ad-libbing a lot of stuff that was meant to be offensive to me. I didn't think it was such a big deal, but John was very protective of me, and he may have had other issues. All of a sudden it was like, 'That's it – I'm going to fire him. I don't have time for this shit.'"

"My feeling was that Bender should be an incredible asshole," recalls Nelson. "I wanted him to be poised for violence from the get-go. So when I started out it was like, 'Whoa! That's too much!'"

"I thought we had to be really careful that Bender not become someone we hate," explains Hughes. "Judd wanted to push him out, and I had to keep bringing him back."

The rest of the cast became concerned that their friend was about to be fired and so they all confronted Hughes. Eventually, Hughes and Nelson worked through their problems, although Nelson continued to tease Ringwald on set.

In his next film, *St Elmo's Fire*, Nelson played yuppy philanderer Alec Newbury.

However, Nelson's career quickly nose-dived after the success of 1985. Following the two group movies came Nelson's stint as a voice-over artist for *Transformers: The Movie* (1986) – he was the voice of Hot Rod. Next came *Blue City* (1986), which reunited him with Ally Sheedy for the third time. As Billy

Turner, he was yet another obnoxious smart ass who returns home to investigate his father's murder. *From the Hip* (1987) was even worse. Bob (*Porky's*) Clark teamed Nelson – as high-flying lawyer Robin 'Stormy' Weathers – with John Hurt as his client. Hurt acted. Nelson overacted. Then, in the television movie *Billionaire Boys Club* (1987), Nelson was back as the despicable young man again – this time as a man who cons rich kid investors. Two years later, Nelson was a serial killer in *Relentless* (1989) and surely must have been tiring of all of these clichéd psycho characters.

Interestingly, he appeared in Mario Van Peebles' controversial 'Black Pack' movie *New Jack City* (1991), a film which focused on the fine art of drug trafficking.

The most interesting film Nelson appeared in, however, was *The Dark Backward* (1991) in which he played a stand-up comedian who gets to make a comeback when a third arm amazingly grows out of his back. But mostly, Nelson spent much of the 90s in television movies (apart from his role in *Airheads* in 1994) and has been best known recently for his regular role as Jack Richmond in the Brooke Shields US television sitcom *Suddenly Susan* (1996–99). He left the series to play the title role in the made-for-television movie *Mr Rock 'n' Roll: The Alan Freed Story* (1999).

SEAN PENN
Born 17 August 1960
Santa Monica, California

"You tolerate me, you really tolerate me."
Sean Penn, accepting his Independent Spirit Award

Sean Penn is best summed up by one of his early movies, *Bad Boys* (1983), in which he plays Mick O'Brien, an angry, hostile 16-year-old sliding into crime. In the first scene he breaks a window of a car and steals a woman's purse. Eventually, his life of petty crime comes to an end when he is involved in a shoot-out in which a gang leader's brother accidentally gets killed. He ends up in a jail for juvenile offenders and must suffer the abuses of his fellow inmates, an assortment of druggies, murderers and rapists. In this lead role, Penn is at his sullen, unlikeable best – impressive, both physically and emotionally. The character he played proved to be one of many bad boy roles the scrawny but tough-looking actor would take on. But in real life, with much publicised bar brawls, encounters with the paparazzi and a stormy marriage with Madonna, his off-screen antics seemed just as interesting, scoring as many headlines as those about his own film career.

Penn was the second of three sons to the television and film director Leo Penn and the actress Eileen Ryan, who retired when he was born. His younger, beefier brother Chris became an actor (*Reservoir Dogs*, *Pale Rider*, *Footloose*), while his older brother Michael carved a successful career out of singing and song-writing. The family lived in a posh part of Santa Monica near to Martin Sheen's home. The Penn boys hung around with the Sheen boys (Charlie and Emilio) during their school years, occasionally dabbling in some Super-8 filmmaking.

Penn originally planned a career in law, but got interested in the film business through his father, opting to forego college in order to spend two years studying at the Los Angeles Group Repertory Theatre, where he worked backstage, as well as making a couple of minor appearances and directing a one-act play,

Terrible Jim Fitch. He then took acting lessons from well-known coach Peggy Feury and broke into television with a small role in the detective series *Barnaby Jones*. After a few more appearances in drama series and made-for-television movies, Penn left California to join the New York acting scene instead. He found work on the Broadway stage (in a production of *Heartland*) and landed his first movie role as Timothy Hutton's room-mate in *Taps* (1981). Set in a military academy, Harold Becker's film gave Penn the chance to shine in a solid first role. His career advanced rapidly as a result.

When Cameron Crowe's novel *Fast Times at Ridgemont High* became a film in 1982 (directed by Amy Heckerling), it gave breaks to a host of young actors including Judge Reinhold, Nicholas Cage, Forest Whitaker, Jennifer Jason Leigh and, most notably, Sean Penn, who was a big hit with audiences as the stoned semi-dropout surfer dude, Jeff Spicoli. Chances are you'll remember this classroom hero for calling Ray Walson "a dick" or for wrecking Charles Jefferson's car. Penn became a potential next big star of Hollywood.

After the offbeat delinquent role in *Bad Boys* (1983), Penn then tried comedy with Donald Sutherland in *Crackers* (1984) and romance in Richard Benjamin's war-time drama *Racing With the Moon* (1984). In fact it was his involvement in this last film which started his problem with the tabloid press. After acting in the film, he then refused to do any publicity because he was busy on another project. This led to stories that he was a pain and a troublemaker who'd been trying to persuade fellow *Racing With the Moon* actor Elizabeth McGovern into saying no to publicity work as well. "Totally bogus," stated Penn. "There wasn't time to allow me to participate in the publicity for the movie… I was doing what I wanted to do – I was acting. I was trying to do the best job that I could."

From then on, Penn developed a reputation for being violent towards the paparazzi. One of his attacks was particularly vicious. In the summer of 1985, the star attacked the small and portly British tabloid photographer Ian Martin-Smith at close range – with a brick. Penn inflicted serious injuries on the photographer, which could easily have been life-threatening had the fit young actor not been pulled off him. The cause of the outburst? No one really knows. It simply seems the sight of a flashbulb set him off.

In John Schlesinger's *The Falcon and the Snowman* (1985), Penn played a nervy, drugged-up young American who, together with sidekick Timothy Hutton, decide to attempt to sell government secrets to the USSR. However, it was his next movie which proved more memorable. *At Close Range* (1986) was based on the true story of the Johnson Gang, who made money from stealing tractors in Pennsylvania in the late 70s. Starring Penn and brother Chris, the film also features Kiefer Sutherland and is scripted by Nicholas Kazan (*Reversal of Fortune*), son of Elia. In fact, most involved were plucked from the loins of the great and good in Hollywood – though this is all pure coincidence, of course. The title song for James Foley's film was specially composed by Madonna. Foley directed her in *Who's That Girl* the following year, although let's not hold that against him. Apart from the flashy, distracting camera work, *At Close Range* is generally an engaging film, with strong performances from both Penn (senior) and Christopher Walken as the Penn boy's outlaw psychopath father.

A meeting between Penn and Madonna during the shooting of *At Close Range* led to a stormy three-year marriage, endless tabloid headlines about the pair and the worst movie of his career. In fact, *Shanghai Surprise* (1986) in which Madonna co-starred, was the only film he made during his marriage. At their wedding, Penn reportedly became so infuriated by press helicopters hovering above the ceremony that he began firing a gun into the air. Penn has never denied this.

Six months into the marriage, Penn took a swing at Daniel Wolinski after the songwriter kissed his wife. He ended up behind bars, serving 32 days in Los Angeles County jail. Penn then violated probation by lashing out at two photographers he caught snooping around his apartment in New York. Penn and Madonna broke up: "It just didn't work out," he said.

Penn's comeback was *Colors* (1988), in which he played a hot-headed rookie coupled with Robert Duvall's veteran cop, assigned to control gang violence in the barrios and ghettos of Los Angeles. Dennis Hopper's film is an unbiased look at a serious real-life problem, plumbing the depths without over-sentimentality. It's one of Penn's best performances. Behind the scenes, however, Penn was in trouble again. An extra on the set of *Colors* took his picture without asking permission. Penn couldn't resist pouncing on the photographer and beating him to the ground. He then ended up serving a 60-day jail term after a subsequent reckless driving charge. On release, Hopper's film was also stirring up trouble because of fears it would encourage more real violence on the streets of LA. Many cinemas refused to screen it and protesters staged demonstrations outside cinemas in New York. Back in LA, a teenager was shot dead while queuing to see it.

Next, Hollywood's bad boy had a small role in his father's film *Judgement in Berlin* (1988), as a German defector. He also played the deranged sergeant in Brian De Palma's *Casualties of War* (1989), but the film came too late in the spate of Vietnam-based pics and the strangely sentimental epilogue did the film no favours, either. Penn then tried comedy again with *We're No Angels* (1990), playing an escaped convict masquerading as a priest with his real-life buddy Robert DeNiro. The gutsy *State of Grace* (1990) had Penn playing a young Irish American returning to his New York roots, alongside a trio of stars – Ed Harris, Gary Oldman and Robin Wright. Wright became his real life girlfriend, then his wife in 1996 and gave him two kids: Dylan Frances and Hopper Jack.

By the early 1990s, Penn had fallen out of love with acting. He announced his retirement from the profession, saying he decided he wanted to spend more time out of the media glare and instead work behind the camera: "I don't like any directors. I don't get along with any of them. Mostly I think their a bunch of whiny people without any point of view. So I don't want to be around them at 6 o'clock in the morning with make-up on. And I'm probably the same way for actors on my set – but that's their problem." Here, Penn was talking during the filming of his own directorial debut, *The Indian Runner* (1991), a raw, moody movie with virtually no plot but loads of good visual ideas from Penn. Inspired by Bruce Springsteen's song *Highway Patrolman*, the film is an examination of the tortured relationship between a thoughtful small-town Nebraska cop Joe

(David Morse) and his irresponsible brother, Vietnam vet Frank (Viggo Mortensen). Although it lacked the eye of a good editor, Penn's debut film was an honourable first effort, if not a box-office success.

For three years, Penn turned down all acting offers – until the right pay cheque came along. He played Al Pacino's lawyer friend in Brian De Palma's *Carlito's Way* (1993) and later played a death-row prisoner in Tim Robbins' acclaimed drama *Dead Man Walking* (1995), for which he received Best Actor prize at both the Berlin Festival and Independent Spirit Awards, as well as an Academy Award nomination. Penn has also had cameos in *Hugo Pool* (1997) and *The Game* (1997), as well as a great star turn in Oliver Stone's *U-Turn* (1997) and a role in the Terence Malick comeback project, *The Thin Red Line* (1998).

Such acting work helps Penn to finance his own filmmaking, although many hope he'll rediscover a love for acting instead. *At Close Range* director James Foley is typical in his opinion: "Sean is one of the greats. And it's a shame he's become a director, because there are too many directors out there, but not enough actors of his calibre."

Since *The Indian Runner*, he's directed *The Crossing Guard* (1995), which starred Jack Nicholson and David Morse as two men coming to terms with the death of a young girl. Marlon Brando reportedly wrote to Penn saying, "*The Crossing Guard* wiped me out. I was in tears." Penn has also directed *Autumn of the Patriarch* (1999), which received critical acclaim.

However, his directing has yet to create blockbuster status. After a somewhat turbulent life, his frustration with performing has resulted in a more mellowed Penn periodically renouncing acting, although he never quite manages to keep his vows to give up.

ALLY SHEEDY
(Alexandra Elizabeth Sheedy)
Born 12 June 1962
New York City

Ally Sheedy, despite appearing in both *the* classic Brat Pack features, never really went along with the lifestyle, choosing to shun the Hollywood parties and the tabloid attention.

The daughter of a literary agent mother and advertising executive father, Sheedy is the eldest of three children. Her parents always encouraged her to be creative and by the age of 12 she had written and published a children's book, *She Was Nice to Mice*, which became a best-seller. She later wrote articles for newspapers, including *The New York Times*. A few years later, Sheedy began acting in television commercials as well as high-school stage productions. She enrolled at the University of Southern California and managed to combine her studies with roles in a number of television movies, including *Splendor in the Grass* (1981), and an on–off role in the hit drama *Hill Street Blues*.

Her feature film debut came as Sean Penn's trusting girlfriend in *Bad Boys* (1983). This led to another teenager girlfriend role (this time she was Jennifer – the computer whizz-kid Matthew Broderick's partner in crime) in John Badham's *WarGames* (1983).

After failing to get the Molly Ringwald role in *Sixteen Candles*, Sheedy auditioned for Hughes again a year later for *The Breakfast Club*. "When I read for *Sixteen Candles*, I was working backstage in a play at USC," recalls Sheedy. "A board had fallen and hit me on the head, and I had two black eyes, but I still really wanted to read. John said he remembered that image of me, and he called me after he saw *WarGames*."

Sheedy breezed through the audition and arrived on set to meet her fellow actors: "Everything sort of evolved into camps," she says. "Molly and Michael were in school a lot, and they knew each other from before. Judd and Emilio became very good friends, and they would all be laughing and running around, playing basketball in the gym or something. I just kind of hung out by myself."

"Allison was very close to me," admits Sheedy. "She looked on the outside the way she felt on the inside, this nondescript dark shape floating around. There are parts of John

Hughes that I incorporated into her. He has a particular way of looking at people sometimes; you can tell he's thinking you're a complete asshole. I had also just worked with Sean Penn on *Bad Boys*, and there's a lot of Sean in Allison – ribbons of things. I've never told him that. Originally, Allison wasn't wearing any make-up in the movie, and at the end Claire put make-up on her. I didn't want it to be a makeover scene, as if somebody painted a face on Allison and suddenly she became acceptable. But I thought if she wore this heavy black eyeliner, then it would be like wiping off the mask to reveal the person underneath. I could have done without the bow in the hair, but it was a compromise."

"Ally had such an aura," recalls Anthony Michael Hall. "She loves books, old music, Bob Dylan. At the time, she was a big fan of Edie Sedgwick and the whole Warhol period. She was kind of ahead of herself in her eclectic palette of tastes. Ally, to this day, is like an older sister to me."

Molly Ringwald has also piled on the praise: "I thought Ally was really beautiful. She was everything that I wasn't. My face is kind of soft; hers is very angular. She had long hair, and I had short hair. I thought she was very sophisticated because she grew up in Manhattan, and she was wonderful about introducing me to things, talking to me about literature. I instantly liked her."

Despite being labelled a Brat Packer because of Hughes' film, Sheedy is still glad she was involved with *The Breakfast Club*: "We were filming all day, and when we got to the line 'When you grow old, your heart dies,' I wanted it to come from the absolute purest place. And all this grief just welled up, this sadness about these people that I loved… and it was almost over. John gave us each a piece of the banister from the library. I still have this little piece of wood. Even though the movie ended, I have this lifeline that I love, especially with Emilio and Judd."

After her role as Gene Hackman and Ellen Burstyn's daughter in the divorce drama *Twice in a Lifetime* (1985), Sheedy re-teamed with Estevez and Nelson for *St Elmo's Fire*. Schumacher explains why he cast Sheedy: "You could not meet Ally and not fall in love with her. She was the girl most likely to succeed." And succeed she did – initially. But the whole Brat Pack scenario was no good for the actress in the long run, and Sheedy could see the probable trajectory of her career early on: "A few people were in that group but broke out of it, like Tom Cruise and Sean Penn, who was always going his own way. But I was right in that cluster. It was a particular genre of movie – young people, in high school or college or just out of college. But then we all started getting older. And there was a glut of those movies and nobody wanted to see them any more. And I had a very hard time moving out of that kind of movie. It became like a horrible rock on my head that I was just trying to lift off, and I didn't know who dropped it there. And for a long time I thought, 'This is what I deserve, because I was successful too young. I have to go through this.'"

After *St Elmo's Fire*, she returned to director John Badham for *Short Circuit* (1986), which revolved around a top-secret weapon-robot called Number Five. The film was a box office success. Sheedy then turned down the Kelly McGillis role in *Top Gun* and instead opted for another role opposite a robot.

This time, the robot's name was Rob Lowe and the film was *Oxford Blues* (1987). *Blue City* (1987), in which she re-teamed with Judd Nelson, was even more of a disaster. Nevertheless, Sheedy picked up the biggest pay cheque she's ever had for her next movie

Maid to Order (1987), in which she played a rich, spoiled Beverly Hills brat who ends up on the streets. The film bombed and it was two years before Sheedy was back on the big screen, as a newspaper reporter in the civil rights drama *Heart of Dixie* (1989).

Sheedy's career was on the slide. She took the role of a psychic drawn into the disturbing mind of a serial killer in a made-for-cable television thriller *Fear* (1990), before re-teaming with Molly Ringwald for Alan Alda's *Betsy's Wedding* (1990), in which she played Alda's daughter. But the film, made the year she'd turned down the lead role in *Wild Orchid* (1990), failed to relaunch her career. People started to take notice again after her role in the John Candy romantic comedy *Only the Lonely* (1991), but by this time, Sheedy was desperately trying to control an addiction to the sleeping pill Halcion, which began during a brief relationship with Bon Jovi guitarist Richie Sambora. After some time in rehab, Sheedy moved back to New York, where she made her off-Broadway debut in *Advice From a Caterpillar* and then wed the actor David Lansbury (Angela's nephew) in 1992. A few years earlier, she'd been a bridesmaid at Demi Moore's wedding – but later told the *New York Times* that Moore's 1991 birthday party event, for which Willis had rented an entire amusement park, served as a "wake-up call" – "I just didn't fit into her world anymore," Sheedy said. Around this time, she was turned down for a role in *A League of Their Own* because she couldn't play baseball well enough. Instead she appeared opposite a genetically mutated dog – in *Man's Best Friend* (1993) – as news reporter-animal rights advocate Lori Tanner.

"I was sitting down trying to figure out why I wasn't considered as a viable alternative for these scripts," explains Sheedy. "How come I couldn't get a meeting with a director? Then it started getting worse – even the casting director wouldn't see me. Why not? 'Well, you know, they think you're really a lightweight actress because you did all those lightweight movies.' I'd say, 'I can do a lot more than that, I just need to get in the door and read.' 'Well, the other problem is that they're looking for something else.' 'What?' 'Someone they want to fuck.' I've heard that over and over again. 'So-and-so wants someone he'd want to fuck. He doesn't want to fuck you, so…' I think you have to prostitute yourself. And if you don't want to, I think you suffer for it. I didn't do it. I have friends who have slept with a lot of people and had relationships with married people who put them in better positions for work. They've gone to parties and met those soulless people…"

Sheedy had a daughter called Rebecca in 1994 and just as she had resigned herself to spending most of her time caring for her (things looked so bad even her own agent dumped her), she began to get work again. She took a small role in *One Night Stand* (1995), but it was her performance as Lucy Berliner, an enigmatic lesbian, drug-taking photographer in the hit independent film *High-Art* (1998) which won her some of the best reviews of her entire career. Critics loved the film and Sheedy began to get decent offers, including her role as a production designer called Liz in *Sugar Town* (1999), a witty satire on the lifestyles of LA's ageing rock-stars.

In the mid-80s, everybody loved Ally Sheedy. But she's also seen the other side – "the absolutely horrific experience, when nobody wants to know your name" – and now prefers to work outside the system and outside the big business of Hollywood. And it's definitely a choice she's made because Sheedy could've easily tried to develop a sex-object image to improve her marketability, but she decided against tight shirts and breast implants…

CHARLIE SHEEN
(Carlos Irwin Estevez)
Born 3 September 1965
New York City

"[Studios] won't hire you, even though you screwed the same whores and ate the bullet for it. Yet they pull you aside at a party and say you're their hero for the things you do." (*Variety* – August 14, 1997)

If it was just his three main Brat Pack movie appearances (*Red Dawn*, *Ferris Bueller's Day Off* and *Young Guns*) being considered for entry into the main players list, Charlie Sheen may not have made it. But the fact that he's the brother of the Pack's unofficial leader, Emilio Estevez, and that he's been Hollywood's worst-behaved actor (the catalogue of crazed incidents is detailed later) definitely mark out Sheen as a true Brat – a party animal who was certainly one of the Pack.

While Emilio proudly chose to keep his original family name, Charlie (once Carlos) preferred to stick with the easier route, adopting his father Martin's showbiz name Sheen and letting the world know he was another second-generation Hollywood son. His other siblings also went on to achieve success in the movie business: his sister Renee Estevez appeared in *Heathers* and *Marked for Murder,* while his other brother Ramon Estevez appeared in *Common Ground* and *Beverly Hills Brats* (produced by Martin's wife, Janet). Their Uncle Joe also became an actor, starring in *Double Blast* and *One Shot Sam*.

Charlie Sheen grew up watching his father on film sets and began making Super-8 home movies of his own very early on. At the time, he'd hang around with childhood buddies Rob Lowe and Sean Penn and his big brother Emilio. "I grew up in Hollywood and there was really nothing else I ever thought about doing," he explains. At the age of nine, he made his debut, appearing with his father (surprise, surprise) in the television movie *The Execution of Private Slovik* (1974), about the first serviceman to be executed for desertion since the Civil

War. A year later he was an extra in *Apocalypse Now*, although when the film's star, Martin Sheen, had a heart attack during filming, Sheen Jr decided not to make acting his career. Instead he began to harbour dreams of pitching for a baseball team. But, at the same time, he was getting into all sorts of trouble. He was arrested for credit-card fraud, possession of marijuana and at school he got caught buying exam answers and later assaulted a teacher. His behaviour put an end to any chance of getting anywhere with baseball and it wasn't long before he turned back to acting. Unfortunately for him, the movie he ended up in – *Grizzly II: The Predator* (1983) – was never released. His next, however, John Milius' gung-ho action flick *Red Dawn* (1984) not only got a full theatrical release but was a big commercial success. Sheen played one of the young American students who do their best to resist a Russian invasion of the USA. Around this time, the young actor's private life started to come under scrutiny when he ditched Paula Profit, the mother of his unborn child.

A decade after Sheen Senior had starred in Terence Malick's acclaimed *Badlands* (1973), Charlie starred (with Maxwell Caulfield) in a similarly brutal tale of two teens on a killing spree – Penelope Spheeris' *The Boys Next Door* (1983). As two ordinary but disaffected kids who vent their rage through murder, both actors are a revelation. But Martin Sheen reportedly hated the film, although that didn't stop the two working together on the television movie *Out of the Darkness* (1985) – Martin in the lead role of Ed Zigo, the New York detective who investigated the 'Son of Sam' murder cases and Charlie way, way down the billing as 'Man Having a Shave'!

Next came Sheen's first lead role, in Mike Marvin's car chase movie *The Wraith* (1986). He played bad boy biker Jake, who doubles as leather-clad drag racer The Wraith after dark. All in all, a strange, supernatural kind a guy. Very odd. Sheen's funny cameo as a punk philosopher in John Hughes' *Ferris Bueller's Day Off* (1986), however, got him noticed: "The first time I really felt like people really knew who I was when I picked up *MAD* magazine and they were doing a parody of Ferris Bueller and there I was in the artwork. Some artist interpreted the character I played in the film. I thought, "This is kind of cool." *MAD* magazine, a magazine I grew up worshipping, and they've got my ugly ass in there gracing the pages. Forget the Oscars, forget all the hoopla, that really stood out for me."

After his brother Emilio turned down the lead in Oliver Stone's next project, Sheen was offered the role instead. The film was *Platoon* (1986) and it made him a star. Sheen shines as a young soldier fighting on the Cambodian border, but Willem Dafoe stole the picture as the sympathetic sergeant. Nevertheless, Stone also cast Sheen in his next film, *Wall Street* (1987), as Buddy Fox, a naïve young broker who sells his soul to the cut-throat capitalist devil (personified by Michael Douglas) and then gets his comeuppance. But once again, Sheen is upstaged: all the glory went to Douglas as the blood-sucking Gordon 'Greed is Good' Gekko, including the Best Actor Oscar. *Wall Street* was another big hit and Sheen began to taste the sweet smell of success – money, cars, wild parties, women and… more women. He even kept a list of 'hot' women with star ratings by each name and confessed to a $50,000 account with the Los Angeles madam Heidi Fleiss (who was later sentenced to three years in jail). Among the many female admirers were Eddie Murphy's ex, Charlotte Lewis, hardcore porn actress Ginger Lynn Allen and Kelly Preston. He even got engaged to Preston, but it all fell through when he accidentally shot her in the arm (his gun apparently fell off the bathroom cabinet in her Hollywood home). She left him and married John Travolta.

Movies that followed *Platoon* and *Wall Street* were not as successful. Sheen was miscast as a car thief in *No Man's Land* (1987), John Sayles' *Eight Men Out* (1988) was hardly seen and, due to an injury, he was forced to pull out of Ridley Scott's *Johnny Utah* (later made as *Point Break* with Keanu Reeves in the role). Luckily, thanks to a helping hand from Emilio, Sheen was cast as Young Gun Brewer in the Brat Pack ensemble movie *Young Guns* (1988). The baseball comedy *Major League* (1989) was also a hit. But then his career slumped again when he played Peter the goatherd in the Heidi update, *Courage Mountain* (1989), and appeared in *Navy SEALS* (1990). Sheen was then on the trail of the bad guys in *The Rookie* (1990) as Clint Eastwood's rich-kid partner. Neither *Men At Work* (1990) directed by Emilio, nor *Stockade* (1990) directed by Martin Sheen did anything to halt the slide.

But then came the Top Gun parody *Hot Shots* (1991), by far Sheen's most successful movie. Two years later, he returned as Topper Harley in the sequel, *Hot Shots – Part Deux* (1993), a witty send-up of Rambo. A cameo in *National Lampoon's Loaded Weapon 1* followed before Disney's *The Three Musketeers* (1993) – which teamed Sheen with Kiefer Sutherland and Chris O'Donnell – went on to make over $100 million world-wide. Things seemed to be looking up.

However, Sheen then decided to turn down lead roles in both *White Men Can't Jump* and *Indecent Proposal* and accepted roles in various boys-and-their-toys flicks such as *Terminal Velocity* (1994). By the late 1990s, he was appearing in lame cash-in films like *The Arrival* (1996), one of the many 'we're not alone' movies which went straight to video. Sheen's personal life was also suffering and his marriage to the model Donna Peele ended after just 14 months. At this point it was reported that he was unable to leave his house without several painkillers and a bottle of Jack Daniels. A month after his divorce, in December 1996, Sheen was arrested for assaulting a woman at his home in Agoura. The woman claimed she was pushed to the floor and knocked out. Then, two months later, on 21 February 1997, he was charged with misdemeanour battery against his ex-girlfriend Brittany Ashland.

Sheen's private life just seemed to get messier. In May 1998 he was rushed to hospital in California after taking a drug overdose. After being released, he checked into a rehab centre but only stayed for one day. Police later pulled him over and arrested him for using medications and drinking. Doctors ordered him to go back to the rehab centre and Sheen was finally put on probation for drugs offences until June 2000.

Amazingly, despite all that the new millennium witnessed a career-boosting cameo for Charlie Sheen – in Spike Jonze's acclaimed *Being John Malkovich* (2000). He's cemented his comeback by being chosen to replace Michael J Fox as the lead character in the TV series *Spin City*.

KIEFER SUTHERLAND
(Kiefer William Frederick Dempsey George Rufus Sutherland)
Born 18 December 1966
London, England

Bearing a striking resemblance to his actor father Donald, Kiefer Sutherland had wanted to follow in his footsteps since early in his childhood. In the first seven years of his professional acting career, he'd made twice as many films, married and divorced the actress Camilia Kath and got engaged to and been ditched by Julia Roberts.

The twin brother of Rachel by Donald Sutherland's second marriage, he was born in London, where his Canadian parents had done their drama training. After his father had struck lucky with the role of Hawkeye in Robert Altman's anti-war film *M.A.S.H.* (1969), the family settled permanently in California when Kiefer was four years old. Shortly after moving, his parents separated – Donald had fallen in love with Jane Fonda, who had participated with him in the anti-Vietnam War troop show *F.T.A.* (Free The Army) while his wife left to join the radical activist group the Black Panthers (she was later arrested for having supplied them with hand grenades). Kiefer remembers the period well: "I remember marching with my mother in Watts at the time of the Watts riots… I remember we had everybody at our house – Black Panthers, a rehab group for people coming out of San Quentin, bikers from all over…"

At 10, Sutherland left for boarding school in Toronto, where he took part in theatre workshops. After a bit part in *Max Dugan Returns* (1983) – which starred his father – he landed his first lead role at 18, in Daniel Petrie's *The Bay Boy* (1984). He played Daniel Campbell, a teenager yearning to be a man in 30s Nova Scotia – but the film was criticised for its needless brutality. Around the same time, Sutherland turned down a role on a soap opera and instead appeared in a jeans television commercial which paid for him to buy a car and drive to LA. When he got there he accepted a role in the television series *Amazing Stories*. The episode he appeared in (*The Mission* directed by Steven Spielberg) was released theatrically overseas. Next, Sutherland took a minor role opposite Sean Penn and Mary Stuart Masterson in *At Close Range* (1986), James Foley's film about a teenager's relationship with his criminal father. However, it was in Rob Reiner's highly successful *Stand By Me*

(1986) that Sutherland grabbed everyone's attention as the bad boy who taunts River Phoenix. A television movie followed – *The Brotherhood of Justice* (1986) – which teamed him with Keanu Reeves as students who help form a vigilante group against the scum element in their school.

After a starring role in the schmaltzy romance *Crazy Moon* (1986), Sutherland appeared in Rick King's low-budget thriller *The Killing Time* (1987), a film produced by Camelia Kath. Her first husband had killed himself in a game of Russian roulette and, despite being 12 years younger, Sutherland fell in love, moved in with her and her 11-year-old son and later got hitched. At the same time, he was vamping it up in Joel Schumacher's latest film: "Sleep all day, party all night, it's fun to be a vampire". The glossy teen pic *The Lost Boys* (1987) had Kiefer Sutherland as a Billy Idol-style villain called David, who makes vampires of missing children – Star (Jami Gertz) and Michael (Jason Patric) amongst others.

After roles in *Promised Land* (1988) and *1969* (1988) came Sutherland's second real Brat Pack movie, the youth western *Young Guns* (1988) in which he co-starred with Estevez, Sheen and Lou Diamond Phillips as the nice guy of the ensemble. After his role as the scheming drug pusher in the Michael J Fox vehicle *Bright Lights, Big City* (1988), he re-teamed with Lou Diamond Phillips in the cop-thriller *Renegades* (1989) and again in *Young Guns II – Blaze Of Glory* (1990), which was even slicker than its MTV-styled original. Another hit followed – Joel Schumacher's *Flatliners* (1990) – which grossed over $10 million in its opening weekend. He co-starred with Julia Roberts and Kevin Bacon as medical students who have to face up to the consequences of experimenting with immortality.

Sutherland's next film, however – *Article 99* (1990) – bombed. Meanwhile, he'd left his wife and child and hooked up with *Flatliners* co-star Julia Roberts. The pair were due to marry on 14 June 1991, but then Roberts discovered he'd been having an affair with a stripper called Amanda Rice. Roberts was hospitalised during work on Steven Spielberg's *Hook* (1991) and a week before the wedding (after all the invitations had been sent out) she cancelled the whole event at an estimated cost of around $500,000. Then, on what was to be the big day, she ran away to Ireland – accompanied by one of Sutherland's best pals, Jason Patric (they'd co-starred in *The Lost Boys*). Patric later moved in with Roberts, which reportedly left Sutherland in tears.

Sutherland then only managed a brief cameo in David Lynch's cult movie *Twin Peaks: Fire Walk With Me* (1992) and was fifth-billed in *A Few Good Men* (1992). His next movie, *The Vanishing* (1993) also bombed, but *The Three Musketeers* (1993) grossed over $100 million worldwide. This success was slightly marred when he got caught drink-driving and was fined £1000 and ordered to do 10 days community service.

In 1993, Sutherland made his directorial debut with a made-for-cable prison drama *Last Light*, in which he also played a killer on Death Row. The film was received well and led to his follow-up directorial effort *Truth Or Consequences N.M.* (1996). Having grown more and more like his father – Sutherland junior has slowed down slightly and, like dad, grown to specialise in slightly sadistic cameo roles – he's also reportedly got closer emotionally. In a recent interview, Donald Sutherland smiled as he told of how his son (now shooting a television pilot in Los Angeles) had been visiting him, trying to get him to start watching his own movies such as a DVD of *Don't Look Now*. Like his father, it seems Kiefer has also mellowed.

MARE WINNINGHAM
(Mary Megan Winningham)
Born 6 May 1959
Phoenix, Arizona

Mare Winningham is usually overlooked when it comes to discussing the Brat Pack. She's become the forgotten one. Admittedly, she was by no means a wild party animal and she only starred in one key Brat Pack movie, but *St Elmo's Fire* was a major part of Brat Pack history.

She was born in Phoenix, Arizona but grew up in California. As a teenager, Winningham studied acting at summer workshops at California State Northridge. She also got involved in school productions at Chatsworth High in Los Angeles with fellow student Kevin Spacey. During their senior year, Spacey played von Trapp and Winningham played Maria in a production of *The Sound of Music*. (In a side story, when she heard about Spacey's Oscar nomination in 1996, she sent him a telegram saying: "Captain von Trapp – congratulations on your nomination – Maria.") Also in her last year at college, she found herself an agent and landed a role in the television movie *The Young Pioneers* (1976) and its sequel *Young Pioneers' Christmas* (also 1976). When she appeared on the American television show *The Gong Show* in 1978, she went under the stage name of Sharon Shamus, playing guitar and singing the Lennon and McCartney hit *Here, There and Everywhere*. She didn't get gonged – the panel loved her. And Winningham always kept an interest in singing and song-writing, even releasing a couple of folk albums.

She had a substantial role in the made-for-television thriller *Special Olympics* (1978), which led to constant television work throughout the 80s. She even won an Emmy award for her role in *Amber Waves* (1980), a film about a New York model thrown into the world of mid-west wheat harvesting, which also starred Kurt Russell and Dennis Weaver.

Then, in 1985, Winningham was cast as the virgin social worker Wendy in *St Elmo's Fire*. The film became a blockbuster, but despite the rest of the gang going on to better things, nothing came along for Winningham. Her character Wendy had not been as interesting (or as glamorous) as the others. While she wore a dowdy pink sweater, Demi Moore's showy character snorted coke and Ally Sheedy got to two-time Judd Nelson with Andrew McCarthy. Winningham ended up back on the television movie circuit – although she did co-star with Tom Hanks in Roger Spottiswoode's hit comedy *Turner and Hooch* (1989), even if the slobbering dog had more scenes.

Things ticked over for the actress until 1995, when it finally looked as though the tables were about to turn. After nearly 20 years in the acting profession, Winningham was nominated for an Oscar for her performance in *Georgia*. None of her old Brat Packer pals had ever been honoured by the Academy, and this was certainly a high-point in an otherwise average career. In the title role, she played a successful country and western artist and the sister of the drug-addicted and alcoholic Sadie (Jennifer Jason Leigh), who's desperate to emulate her. Both actresses did well to portray an essentially unresolvable relationship. More recently, Winningham won her second Emmy for the role of the infamous prison governor Lurleen Wallace, in the television movie *George Wallace* (1998).

The Second Team

KEVIN BACON
Born 8 July 1958
Philadelphia, Pennsylvania

Bacon was born and raised in Philadelphia. At the age of 17, he became the youngest student to appear at the Circle in the Square Theatre in New York. He studied acting at workshops in the city and appeared in the daytime soap operas *Search For Tomorrow* and *Guiding Light*, until he made his feature film debut at 20, as Chip Diller, a preppy fraternity recruit in *National Lampoon's Animal House* (1977). The crude but funny parody of 60s co-ed movies was a big success and secured the futures of newcomers John Belushi, Karen Allen and Tom Hulce – but it didn't have much of an effect on Bacon's career.

Small roles followed in both a Burt Reynolds film *Starting Over* and a Glen Ford television movie *The Gift*, but the young actor was finding more success on the stage with appearances in the off-Broadway productions *Album*, *Poor Little Lambs*, *Getting Out* and *Forty-Deuce*, for which he won an Obie. He made his Broadway debut in 1983 with Sean Penn in *Slab Boys* and later starred in the 1986 Broadway revival of Joe Orton's *Loot*.

Bacon's first real chance to shine on the screen came in Barry Levinson's directorial debut, *Diner*, in 1982. At the drab Baltimore diner, the guys meet to eat fries dunked in brown gravy and discuss their Friday night dates. Bacon gave a memorable performance as the hard-drinking, self-destructive rich-kid Fenwick, who opens the film by staging his own death in a car wreck. His cynical smirk hinted this privileged character was in fact a lot less happy than most of his working class pals, including Eddie (Steve Guttenberg), Shrevie (Daniel Stern) and Boogie (Mickey Rourke). Most of the actors were virtually unknown at the time of the film's release, but became sought-after in the film industry soon after.

In 1984 came *Footloose*, the film which turned Bacon (albeit briefly) into an 80s heart-throb. Herbet Ross's film is *Flashdance* meets *Rebel Without a Cause*, with Bacon as Ren, the new kid in a small town where dancing has been banned by the Puritanical preacher (John Lithgow). Cue teen angst, with Bacon determined to arrange a dance and steal away the preacher's daughter (Lori Singer).

Footloose was a big teen hit, but Bacon failed to consolidate his success and stardom never came. He did, however, deliver a brilliantly quirky performance as Dennis the punky cab driver in *Enormous Changes at the Last Minute* (1985), which received critical acclaim but limited distribution.

Unfortunately, scriptwriter–director John Hughes' long-awaited first grown-up film, *She's Having a Baby* (1988), with Bacon as the terrified and trapped newlywed husband, was a box-office fizzle. Furthermore, Bacon's next two pictures, the thriller *Criminal Law* (1988) and the satire on Hollywood *The Big Picture* (1989) were damned by studios who held their release for some time.

In 1990, Bacon scored with the tongue-in-cheek comic horror flick *Tremors*, which had him as a tough handyman battling with giant worm-creatures. This was a good, quirky, off-the-wall part for Bacon and re-established him as a leading man. In the same year, he co-starred with Kiefer Sutherland in a more serious outing, Joel Schumacher's *Flatliners*, which saw him as one of a group of daring medical students experimenting with death – and living to tell about it. Bacon was originally offered the Sutherland lead role, but opted instead for the more cautious character David Labraccio. A year later, Bacon also impressed critics with his excellent performance as a homosexual convict informer in Oliver Stone's *JFK*. Despite Kevin Costner being top-billed, it was Bacon who got the critics' attention.

More recently, Bacon has starred in such films as *A Few Good Men* (1992), *The River Wild* (1992) – for which he received a Golden Globe nomination – and *Apollo 13* (1995) He reunited with director Barry Levinson for *Sleepers* (1996), in which he played the reform school guard Sean Noakes, among an ensemble of strong male leads (De Niro, Hoffman and Pitt).

Around the same time, Bacon was unexpectedly finding fame in a different business – the world of old-fashioned home entertainment. A company devised a bizarre board game called 'Six Degrees of Kevin Bacon' (based on John Guare's play and film *Six Degrees of Separation*) which involved having to link random names in the movie business to Kevin Bacon within six moves.

Bacon has experienced an uneven career to say the least, even describing himself as "a workhorse actor" who's "here for the long haul". He has already tried his hand at directing with his 1996 film *Losing Chase*, which starred his wife and Helen Mirren. However, married to actress Kyra Sedgewick, he is devoted to his family and has even started a band with his brother. Performing in The Bacon Brothers, he says, is just as enjoyable as acting. He was most recently seen in the thriller *A Stir of Echoes* (1999).

JON CRYER
Born 16 April 1965
New York City

The son of actor David Cryer and actress/songwriter Gretchen, Jon Cryer studied at the Stagedoor Manor Performing Arts Training Centre and at RADA in London. He began his professional acting career on the stage – starring in Neil Simon's autobiographical play *Brighton Beach Memoirs* and in Harvey Fierstein's *Torch Song Trilogy*.

Robert Altman spotted him in the Fierstein production and cast him in the little-seen *OC and Stiggs* (1984) as Paul Dooley's geeky son, whose worst fate is being blasted with water by the movie's two pranksters (Daniel Jenkins and Neill Barry). Very lame. In the same year, Cryer took over from Matthew Broderick in *No Small Affair* (1984). The film began production in 1981 with Broderick and Sally Field starring. However, Martin Ritt called the whole thing off after 10 days, blaming 'exhaustion' on his part. It was all back on three years later with Jerry Schatzberg directing Cryer in the lead role of Charles Cummings, a goofy 16-year-old social misfit interested only in photography. Then he falls in love with singer Laura Victor (Demi Moore), who works in a nearby bar. He makes it his mission to make her famous, putting her picture on billboards all over town. She then gets a record deal and disappears to LA. Cryer was a suitable replacement for Broderick and quickly came to be relied on as just another Hollywood Nice Guy, a rent-a-cutie for teen-movie casting directors. In the John Hughes-scripted *Pretty in Pink*, Cryer was cast as Duckie Dale.

Cryer had a supporting role in the worst in the series of Superman films: *Superman IV The Quest For Peace* (1987) and won lead roles in the high-school comedy *Hiding Out* (1987) and in Penelope Spheeris' particularly unfunny punk western *Dudes* (1987). He also cropped up in Arthur Penn's *Penn and Teller Get Killed* (1988) and had a higher profile role in Jim Abrahams' *Top Gun* spoof, *Hot Shots* (1991). Cryer also has two television sitcom flops to his name – *The Famous Teddy Z* and the *Friends* rip-off, *Partners*.

JOHN CUSACK
Born 26 June 1966
Evanston, Illinois

One of five children, John Cusack is the son of Emmy award-winning documentary film-maker Richard Cusack and brother of actress Joan (*Broadcast News* and *Working Girl*). From the age of nine, John attended the River Theatre Workshop in his home town of Evanston, a posh suburb of Chicago. By the age of 12, he was appearing in corporate videos and commercials for Heinz and McDonald's. While still at high school, Cusack also wrote and staged two musical comedies that eventually aired on a local cable television station. Cusack still lives in Chicago and continues to work in the theatre there, where he has produced *The Day They Shot John Lennon* and directed the plays *Alagazam... After The Dog Wars* and *Methusalem* as well as a stage version of Hunter S Thompson's classic novel *Fear and Loathing in Las Vegas*. However, for a short time in his career, Cusack was part of the Brat Pack party scene, cropping up in a variety of teen movies.

Cusack didn't get on at school. He hated it and rarely attended, once describing himself as having a "chronic rebellion disorder". Luckily for him, he was taken on by Chicago-based agent Ann Geddes, who got him an audition for a part as Rob Lowe's school friend in *Class* (1983), which he got. The film's director, Lewis John Carlino, cast the 16-year-old Cusack in the relatively small role: "Cusack was the sleeper in my film. From the start he was quick, inventive, and knew where he was going. It's been gratifying to see his growth. I see a serious, major talent growing there. But even at the time he displayed that promise."

Cusack also landed parts in a further two feature films in his last school year – *Grandview USA* with Jamie Lee Curtis and *Sixteen Candles* with Molly Ringwald. They were both supporting roles shot during his school holidays and were released in 1984. A year later he graduated to lead roles.

In Rob Reiner's above-average teenage comedy *The Sure Thing* (1985), Cusack played a fun-loving, sex-driven 19-year-old Ivy League student called Gib. Together with his complete opposite, the college square, Alison (Daphne Zuniga), they set out on a quest to find her fiancée and his dream girl in California, only to find that together they are 'the sure thing'. "Have you ever considered a sexual encounter so intense it could conceivably change your political views?" he asked her. Reiner's film foreshadowed the themes of *When Harry Met Sally* and included some great lines for Cusack, resulting in a worthwhile showcase for the young actor.

Also in 85, he played a hobo in the Disney period piece *The Journey of Natty Gann*, followed by another teen role in Savage Steve Holland's *Better Off Dead*, a film which must have been the first to use teen suicide as a source of humour. Cusack is a high-school ski-team hopeful called Lane Myer, whose world collapses when his girlfriend Beth announces, "I think it would be in my best interests if I went out with someone more popular" and does just that by dumping him in favour of ski star Roy Stalin. After numerous botched attempts at suicide, Lane takes on Stalin in a race to the death down the treacherous slopes. It's all hit-and-miss slapstick with Cusack tormented along the way by paperboys, his eight-year-old brother Badger and even his cartoon drawings, which come to life and tell him, "You're a spastic nerdbag!" There is, however, one moment of triumph for Lane, when he sends away for a book advertised on the back of a cereal packet, entitled 'How to Pick Up Trashy Women'. Cut to Lane surrounded by several wild, up-for-it sluts.

After a cameo appearance as Wil Wheaton's older brother in Rob Reiner's *Stand By Me* (1986), Cusack starred in the follow-up Savage Steve Holland movie, *One Crazy Summer* (1986), which also featured Demi Moore. No bikinis this time and the ski race is replaced with a less climactic boat race.

In *Hot Pusuit* (1987), Cusack is a college student again. He plans an exotic holiday with his girlfriend's family, but is grounded because of his bad grades. When he finally takes his holiday of a lifetime he arrives to face incarceration and then encounters desperate hijackers. Absolutely average. 1987 also saw a cameo for him in the acclaimed satire *Broadcast News*.

One of the best youth comedies Cusack starred in was Bill Fishman's *Tapeheads* (1989), which paired him with Tim Robbins. Ivan (Cusack) and Josh (Robbins) are two security guards with a dream. They lose their jobs and become 'The Video Aces', producers of rock videos with attitude. They end up working in downtown LA for Mo Fuzz (Don Cornelius) who says, "There's only one thing that adds real production value... tits and ass!" A copy of one of their videos gets mixed up with a living will video. It becomes a hit and Ivan and Josh get the fame they desperately wanted. Like Rob Reiner's *This Is Spinal Tap*, the humour is based around in-jokes about the politics of the MTV industry.

Cusack was also impressive as a love-struck high-school student called Lloyd Dobler in Cameron Crowe's *Say Anything* (1989). Cusack's Lloyd is a cheerful, sensitive chap in search of an extra-special girl. But this turned out to be the last teen pic he got involved in. He turned down teen roles to avoid typecasting, including saying no to big bucks to star opposite Molly Ringwald in *For Keeps,* and instead he opted for a complete change of direction. He began to work with more serious film-makers such as John Sayles, Roland Joffe and Stephen Frears in the period dramas *Eight Men Out* (1988), *Fat Man and Little Boy* (1989) and *The Grifters* (1990). Frears commented: "John is like a jazz musician. He zones off into these dark moods, then zaps out of it with no warning and goes on. There's a light blackness to his talent that I found extraordinary. Someone once described John to me as being Jimmy Stewart with an edge, and I think that description is quite accurate."

Cusack's subtle, relaxed performances proved he was coming of age: "I've gone through three phases in my life," he says. "The ambitious young actor getting trashed at parties. Then the phase when I began taking myself and my work seriously. I felt enormously self-important and I was a pain to be with. Then the growing-up phase. I've started to see the world with less hostility and I'm no longer as extreme in my behaviour."

During the 90s, Cusack took various cameo roles, including an appearance in Robert Altman's send-up of Hollywood *The Player* (1992), as well as Abbe Wool's *Roadside Prophets* (1992). At the same time he was rejecting lead roles in the likes of *Sleeping With the Enemy* and *White Men Can't Jump*, which were both obvious hits. By far the most interesting of Cusack's appearances in lower budget films was his small role in Peter McCarthy's *Floundering* (1994). McCarthy was already the producer of Alex Cox's *Repo Man* and Bill Fishman's *Tapeheads* (1989) and his own directorial debut was just as culty and surreal. It's a subversive satire set in the wake of the 1992 Los Angeles riots with a group of going-nowhere twentysomethings coming face to face with the chaos around them. Cusack's minor role as a philosophical party-goer is a real winner.

Cusack also turned down starring roles in *Apollo 13* and *Indecent Proposal*, instead choosing more meaningful work in projects such as *Bob Roberts* (1992), *Bullets Over Broadway* (1994) and *Grosse Point Blank* (1997). He scripted and co-produced the latter and wants to get involved further in production. His latest film is *High Fidelity*, directed by Stephen Frears, and based on Nick Hornby's best-seller: "I loved the book and decided to go after the rights myself – I wound up producing the film," he explains. "The film is a male confessional. I don't know why, but I can't help playing that kind of character. I have a need to be different."

Increasingly private, Cusack's flings with leading ladies, including Minnie Driver from *Grosse Point Blank*, have been kept out of the tabloids. He's now reportedly dating *Scream 3* star Neve Campbell – although nowadays he won't be seen out at Hollywood parties. The shy star has now spent 17 years in Hollywood as an actor and writer: "Celebrities are worshipped in society when in fact their private lives are fairly ordinary and unremarkable. I've never let myself get emotionally involved in all the hype of the moment. Every two years or so it's my turn to be the flavour of the month. You have to wade through the crap to find your one shining moment."

JAMI GERTZ
Born 28 October 1965
Chicago, Illinois

Jami Gertz landed her role in the television comedy series *Square Pegs* by winning an American talent contest. After the series, she studied at New York University's Drama School and eventually landed a few parts in the theatre in Los Angeles as well as a few bit parts in movies such as *On The Right Track* (1981), Franco Zeffirelli's *Endless Love* (1981) – which also marked Tom Cruise's film debut (he was eighteenth-billed) and *Alphabet City* (1982). She also had a small role in writer-director John Hughes' *Sixteen Candles* (1984).

Gertz had a bigger role in the teen comedy *Mischief* (1985) and then started getting leads – opposite Kevin Bacon in *Quicksilver* (1986) and as Brat Packer Ralph Macchio's girlfriend in *Crossroads* (1986). She also landed the female lead opposite Jason Patric in the terrible *Mad Max* rip-off *Solarbabies* (1986), although Gertz wasn't impressed with her co-star: "Jason would mumble and wouldn't look me in the face when he talked. Finally I told him I wasn't going to talk to him anymore unless he looked at me. I couldn't believe he was so shy."

Nevertheless, she later re-teamed with Patric in the stage production, *Outta Gas on Lover's Leap* at the Los Angeles Coast Playhouse – and she also played his romantic interest in Joel Schumacher's *The Lost Boys* (1987), the fairly funny tale of contemporary teenagers who happen to be vampires. Gertz is the gorgeous girl in Kiefer Sutherland's band of supernatural bikers and the attraction for Michael Emerson (Patric) who, to win her love, must first become "a creature of the night".

Having become the latest studio starlet, Gertz was then offered the role of Blair, girlfriend of Robert Downey Jr's Julian in Marek Kaniewska's adaptation of Bret Easton Ellis' *Less Than Zero* (1987). This tragic love story has Gertz begging an old flame to save his mate and her new boyfriend from the spiral of drug abuse. Kaniewska's original cast wish-list would have put Downey alongside Kiefer Sutherland and the then-unknown Uma Thurman. Although he did get Downey, Hollywood politics meant James Spader and Jami Gertz replaced Sutherland and

Thurman. At the time, Downey was completely out-of-it off the set. Gertz is amazed he came through the film alive: "The scenes were so true to life. You had the feeling, 'Is what happens to Julian going to happen to Robert?'"

Well, so far it hasn't and Downey still has a career – and a successful one at that. As for Gertz, it seems she is destined to remain one of Hollywood's hangers-on. Without real acting talent, she has had a few high points in her career but, on the whole, never quite made it big or even managed, through sheer luck, to appear in a blockbuster movie. The 90s brought only supporting roles in films like *Renegades* (1990), *Sibling Rivalry* (1990) and most notably her role as Dr Melissa Reeves, Bill Paxton's pretty therapist fiancée in the horror spoof *Twister* (1989). She also made television appearances in episodes of *Dream On* (1990) and lasted a whole season as Dr Nina Pomerantz in *ER* (1994).

JENNIFER GREY
Born 26 March 1960
New York City

The daughter of Broadway actor/dancer/choreographer Joel Grey and his dancer wife Jo, Jennifer achieved most success with the surprise hit of 1987, *Dirty Dancing*. But like many former teen stars, with a mixture of bad choices and bad luck, she saw her career take a nose-dive in the 90s.

Grey was a dedicated dance student in New York and appeared as a dancer in a variety of television commercials while also studying acting at the city's Neighbourhood Playhouse School of Theatre. Grey has always loved the stage and has appeared in the off-Broadway show *Album* as well as in plays at San Francisco's American Conservatory Theatre and the Williamstown Theatre in Massachusetts.

In 1984, Grey made her feature-film debut with a minor role in *Reckless* (1984), another alienated youth movie by James Foley. Another small role followed, this time in Francis Ford Coppola's multi-million dollar spectacular *The Cotton Club* (1984), which centred around Harlem nightlife in the Roaring Twenties (the film featured Richard Gere doing all his own cornet solos – Duke Ellington style). Grey had more to do in John Milius' tough teen fantasy film *Red Dawn* (1984), as one of a group of teenage vigilantes defending America against the Russians from their hideout in the hills. The up-and-coming young cast also featured future *Dirty Dancing* star Patrick Swayze, as well as C Thomas Howell and Charlie Sheen.

Grey's performance in John Hughes' *Ferris Bueller's Day Off* (1986) was a real turn-up for the books. She played the ever so jealous and frustrated sister of Ferris (her then real-life boyfriend, Matthew Broderick) and enjoyed a lot of funny scenes. Ferris' sister was always worse off than her brother, who's the apple of his Mom's eye. Ferris, it seems, can get away with skipping school when he wants, but for Jeannie, it's a different story: "If I was bleeding out my eyes, you guys'd make me go to school," she complains.

Dirty Dancing was the huge sleeper hit of the late 80s. Set in a Jewish Catskills vacation resort in the Sixties, Grey played Francis 'Baby' Houseman, a naïve young holidaymaker who falls for the resident dance instructor Johnny Castle (Patrick Swayze). Of course, soon they both fall in love – cue a few mild bedroom scenes and dirty dances. Audiences loved the sexual chemistry between the two lead stars and women, in particular, fell for new hunk of the month Swayze. The film was turned into a television series, Swayze went on to even bigger stardom and Grey… well, Grey didn't. Instead, she treated herself to a nose job, a mistake because she'd achieved fame based on her plain Jewish American Princess image.

The sequel to *Dirty Dancing* never happened and Grey waited around for two years for the Damon Runyan adaptation *Bloodhounds of Broadway* (1989), about a bunch of 1920s Broadway jazz-babes and hustlers – a film so bad it didn't even get a British release. It was simply a vehicle for Madonna, who played a nightclub singer in love with gambler Randy Quaid. Around this time, rumours started spreading of a lesbian love affair between the pop singer and Grey. In fairness to Grey, it was a publicity-seeking Madonna who had hinted at such a romance with a particularly teasing performance on American television's *Late Night With David Letterman* show.

After *Bloodhounds* flopped and went straight-to-video, Grey took a role in a television movie *Murder in Mississippi* (1990) about the events leading up to the 1964 murders of civil rights workers Schwerner, Goodman and Chaney. The drama was well received and Grey had some good reviews. But, as the old saying goes, why should audiences actually pay to see a star (or former star) at the cinema when they can see them for free on television? Grey's good reviews didn't lead to more roles for the big screen – just more television movie parts.

In 1994, she was cast in a new Gene Wilder television sitcom *Something Wilder*, but was replaced when test audiences disapproved of the two leads' age difference in the pilot episode. Grey then briefly dated President Clinton's Communications Director, George Stephanopolis. After a string of average television movies in the 90s, she's had only a few high profile appearances – most notably one guest spot on *Friends* as Rachel's ex-best friend, Mindy. And her last television series *It's Like, You Know…* (1999) also turned out to be a dud.

C THOMAS HOWELL
Born 7 December 1966
Los Angeles, California

Thomas Howell was a true child star, appearing regularly on the American television series *Little People* by the age of four. More television work followed (*Into the Homeland*, *Two Marriages*) and Howell then made his feature-film debut in Steven Spielberg's *ET* (1982). He was just 16 and played a small role as one of the local neighbourhood kids. The film became one of the most popular of all time and Howell found himself with plenty of scripts to choose from.

He took the lead role in Francis Ford Coppola's classic Brat Pack movie *The Outsiders* (1983). He played Ponyboy, a greaser from the wrong side of town and the alter ego of SE Hinton, the author of the original novel. Howell was perfect for the role: he was cute, shy and sensitive – and he outshone all the other new teen stars in the film (Matt Dillon, Ralph Macchio, Emilio Estevez and Tom Cruise).

Next, he teamed up with fellow-Outsider Patrick Swayze for John Milius' jingoistic *Red Dawn* (1984). Howell really didn't look at home with all this macho nonsense and it was just plain embarrassing to watch him drinking deer blood to prove to Swayze he was a real man. Perhaps that's why he chose to appear in Marvin Chomsky's *Tank* (1984), which ended up as a kind of spoof on *Red Dawn*.

Howell reunited with Swayze for *Grandview, USA* (1984) as two guys both romantically linked with demolition derby owner Jamie Lee Curtis. It was a messy film, but it proved Howell was more at home with comedy. Hence *Secret Admirer* (1985), a slapstick comedy with Howell as Michael Ryan, a teenager who falls for dumb blonde Deborah Ann Fimple (Kelly Preston) and writes a series of love letters with the help of his friend Toni (Lori Loughlin) who acts as a go-between. But the letters end up in the wrong (adult) hands and the farce begins. The comedy continued when Howell played a smug Harvard Law School entrant in Steve Miner's *Soul Man* (1986) who has the smile wiped off his face when daddy decides not to pay his school fees. On hearing that black students get more scholarships, Mark promptly blacks up. An Afro hairstyle and a few bronzing pills seem to do the trick (After all, "This is the

Cosby decade. America loves blacks!"). But Mark bombs out on the basketball court and his cover is blown. Howell got together with his *Soul Man* co-star Rae Dawn Chang, and later they married.

In the sinister slasher movie *The Hitcher* (1986), Howell was Jim Halsey, the lonely motorist trying to stay awake at the wheel. Unfortunately for him, the mysterious stranger he picks up turns out to be a psychotic drifter called John Ryder (Rutger Hauer), who murders those who give him lifts. Jim manages to propel him from the car, but Ryder then succeeds in killing everyone Jim comes into contact with, crimes for which Jim is eventually arrested and jailed. Howell is good as the innocent teen turned hunter and manages to hold enough interest opposite Hauer's memorable psycho.

However, from the late 80s onwards, Howell's career got caught in a downward spiral. He appeared in the disastrous *A Tiger's Tale* (1988) and also co-starred with his wife in *Far Out Man* (1990), a movie by his father-in-law Thomas Chong (of Cheech and Chong fame), who himself admitted it was only 'an attempt' at film-making. "No Brain, No Pain" reads the video cover. Exactly.

Howell did manage to stay in teen roles for a couple more years – for example, as a young vigilante seeking revenge for the murder of his hippy parents in *Kid* (1990) and as a Californian teen seduced by the world of beach volleyball in the fourth-rate jock drama *Side Out* (1990). Adult roles included his inoffensive young stud of an advertising executive in *Dangerous Indiscretion* (1994), an erotic thriller in which he found himself at the mercy of devious business tycoon Malcolm McDowell. But for the rest of the 90s, on the whole Howell's films went straight to video and he was reduced to a string of uninteresting made-for-television movies such as the Canadian cable television-produced thriller *Fatal Affair* (1998), in which a rather weary-looking Howell starred as a prime suspect accused of killing his girlfriend. Howell has also briefly starred in the Aaron Spelling cop vs vampire television show *Kindred: The Embraced*.

Unfortunately for Howell, the teen movies he did so well in disappeared as grown-ups returned to the cinema – and now it's the case of another former teen idol facing up to an uncertain future.

TIMOTHY HUTTON
Born 16 August 1960
Malibu, California

At 19, Timothy Hutton became the youngest actor ever to win an Oscar. His Best Supporting Actor prize was for his anguished performance as a suicidal teenager in Robert Redford's directorial debut, *Ordinary People* (1980). Hutton was also awarded a Golden Globe and a Los Angeles Film Critics' award for his part in Redford's film, an adaptation of an unpublished novel by Judith Guest, a then-unknown housewife from Minnesota. Redford had signed up Hutton after seeing him in the television movie *Friendly Fire* (1979) as the fearful son of a farming family coming to terms with the death of his brother in Vietnam. The film won four Emmys.

Hutton was only two years old when his parents divorced. He moved around the States with his mother before finally settling with her and his sister Heidi in Berkeley, California. At Los Angeles' Fairfax High School, he began to rebel: "My friends and I stole cars from hotel parking lots. We broke into newspaper machines for pocket money. We even got people to leave their cars with us to be washed and we'd take them out for joy rides. I don't glorify or romanticise what we did. It was idiotic and irresponsible."

Once he'd calmed down, Hutton began acting in shows with his father and then landed a string of television parts before being spotted by Robert Redford. Four months after the sad death of his father, from cancer of the liver, Redford chose him for the role of Conrad, a young man haunted by the death of his brother. Conrad's suicidal depression threatens the middle-class harmony of Mary Tyler Moore and Donald Sutherland's happy marriage. Judd Hirsch is the psychiatrist who tries to help. It was a typically liberal domestic drama from Redford, but Hutton showed promise and it looked like he wasn't just another one of the crowd of second-generation Hollywood kids. The Oscar triumph at the 1980 Academy Awards, however, was a one-off. Hutton spent the rest of the decade playing an assortment of wimps without matching his early success.

After another television movie called *A Long Way Home* (1981), in which he played a young man wrenched apart from his brother and sister to be placed in foster care, Hutton landed the role of the rebellious army cadet in Harold Becker's *Taps* (1981). He leads his fellow students, including a young Tom Cruise and Sean Penn, in an armed occupation of their academy, in the hope of preventing its demolition. But when the National Guard is called in, their passive protest predictably turns into a bloodbath. Despite his short back and sides haircut, Hutton still appears too nice for the hardman role – although he did pick up another Golden Globe nomination.

In Sidney Lumet's *Daniel* (1983), Hutton played the title role – the son of a couple executed for passing on secrets to the Russians. But the film was released in the week when a US passenger plane was shot down near North Korea, yet another Cold War 'incident' which put audiences off going to see a leftist picture like Lumet's. Not surprisingly, the film lost out at the box office. In the Canadian produced *Iceman* (1984), Hutton took lessons in the Eskimo language for his role as a scientist based in the Arctic. Again, Hutton was impressive, but the film bombed at the box office. Next, he signed up for MGM's western *Roadshow* in 1983, but the picture was later cancelled. Jack Nicholson, who'd also signed up, received an undisclosed sum from the studio, which overlooked Hutton when handing out compensation. Eventually, he received $2.25 million in compensation and $7.5 million in punitive damages after a lengthy court battle in Los Angeles.

For John Schlesinger's *The Falcon and the Snowman* (1985), Hutton re-teamed with Sean Penn to play two young Americans convicted of selling secrets to the Russians in 1977, while in Bob Clark's *Turk 182* (1985), he played a vigilante graffiti artist who goes to war with the Mayor of New York (Robert Culp).

On New Year's Day 1986, Hutton proposed to his girlfriend Debra Winger, and married her 10 days later. They had a son named Emmanuel Noah Hutton. However, the couple divorced in 1990, and Hutton's career also continued to slide. Alan Rudolph's fantasy film *Made in Heaven* (1987) and Gregory Nava's *A Time of Destiny* (1988) were both mistakes and led to Hutton having to take third billing as Dennis Quaid's nephew in *Everybody's All-American* (1988). In fact, most of Hutton's subsequent appearances were in films which bombed at the box office – including Jerry Skolimowski's tedious Turgenev adaptation *Torrents of Spring* (1990) and Tom Holland's *The Temp* (1993), which had him as a young exec who suspects his secretary of murder.

Hutton's ticket out of straight-to-video hell was in Ted Demme's *Beautiful Girls* (1996), a thirtysomething comedy/drama about a depressed pianist called Willie Conway (Hutton) unable to break the New York music scene. He returns to his isolated home town to visit his weird family, attend a school reunion and decide where to steer his pointless life. According to Demme: "Timmy related to the material immediately and just had a great take on it. He's an amazing actor, so the chance to work with someone like that was exciting to me. Tim brought so many dimensions to the character that were amazing, just from being a confused guy, to being one of the boys, to this really sweet relationship with the girl next door."

Beautiful Girls also brought Hutton back together with his on-and-off girlfriend Uma Thurman, who played a worldly wise career woman in the film. It also led to better parts toward the end of the 90s – opposite David Duchovny in the thriller *Playing God* (1997) and opposite Stephen Dorff and Harvey Keitel in John Irvin's *City Of Industry* (1997).

Everybody in Hollywood knew Timothy Hutton had talent. He had the face, the style, the energy and emotional depth – and he should have been a big star. Yet for much of his career, Hutton has been at a standstill, resigning himself to dud after dud. Nevertheless, he's been clever enough to pursue other strands to his career: so far he's played leads in Broadway stage productions such as the Alec Baldwin role in *Prelude to a Kiss* (1990); he's directed television and video – NBC's *Amazing Stories* and the popular music promo for the Cars hit *Drive* (1984); and, most recently, Hutton has executive-produced a television movie called *Mr and Mrs Loving* (1996), a true story based on a couple who had to go to the Supreme Court in the 1950s to defend their inter-racial marriage.

MARY STUART MASTERSON
Born 28 June 1966
New York City

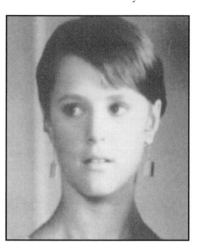

Having started out playing the 'girlfriend' to one male Brat Packer after another, Mary Stuart Masterson could quite easily have become destined to remain just another one of Hollywood's pretty bland young actresses. But her performance as a hot-tempered tomboy in *Some Kind of Wonderful* (1987) proved she had talent.

The daughter of actor-director Peter Masterson (whose directorial debut *The Trip to Bountiful* won Geraldine Page an Oscar in 1985) and Broadway singer Carlin Glynn, Masterson was always mixing with performers and never thought twice about a career in the acting profession. Her film debut came at the age of eight in the quietly chilling *The Stepford Wives* (1975). She played the young daughter of her real father Peter and Katherine Ross. At the same, Masterson was also appearing in school productions at the Dalton School in New York. Time out for such projects didn't hinder her studies – she was always a straight-A student.

After leaving school, Masterson spent the summer in acting workshops at Robert Redford's Sundance Institute. She quickly found herself an agent and soon landed her first role as Andrew McCarthy's girlfriend in *Heaven Help Us* (1985), a film set in 1960s Brooklyn about a bunch of Catholic school kids who keep getting into trouble with the priests. A year later, Masterson found herself as the girlfriend to another Brat Packer – this time to Sean Penn – in James Foley's disturbing and bloody drama, *At Close Range*. Next, she was DB Sweeney's other half in Francis Ford Coppola's sympathetic study of patriotism versus pacifism, *Gardens of Stone* (1987).

Howard Deutch's *Some Kind of Wonderful* (1987) finally allowed Masterson to shine. In the John Hughes-scripted story of teenage love, she plays a drummer/mechanic tomboy called Watts, who's eating her heart out over best friend Eric Stoltz, who thinks he's in love with the far more glamorous – and popular – Lea Thompson. When Keith (Stoltz) wants to ask Amanda (Thompson) out on a date, Masterson offers some advice: "This babe has plenty of battle scars... you should consider whether or not you feel you can deliver a kiss that kills." She then offers herself as a body to practice on. Before the date takes place, she tells Amanda, "Break his heart – I break your face." Much to the delight of everyone, Watts finally wins Keith away from Amanda.

Masterson was one of the main players (alongside Robert Mitchum and Harry Dean Stanton) in *Mr North* (1988), an adaptation of Thornton Wilder's *Theophilus North*, scripted and executive-produced by John Huston. She also had a supporting role in the clumsy romantic comedy *Chances Are* (1989). In the same year, Masterson won rave reviews for her performance in Jonathan Kaplan's *Immediate Family*. She played a young mother who agrees to give away her as-yet-unborn baby for adoption, and then changes her mind at the last minute.

In the not-so-funny *Funny About Love* (1990), Masterson didn't appear until an hour into the film – as Gene Wilder's mistress, and didn't have much more to do in Arthur Hiller's *Married to It* (1991). Shortly afterwards, Masterson moved to Texas to be with her husband while he completed his University Masters degree. It was only a temporary break and she was soon back to taking interesting roles in films such as John Avnet's *Fried Green Tomatoes at the Whistlestop Cafe* (1991), in which she played the irrepressibly daredevilish tomboy Idgie Threadgoode opposite Mary-Louise Parker's demure and good-hearted Ruth. Together they run the Whistle Stop Cafe – a railside eatery serving up good old southern food, friendship, laughter and occasional murder. The film was a surprise hit, grossing over $81 million in the USA. This led to a co-starring role opposite Johnny Depp in the off-the-wall indie hit *Benny and Joon* (1993). Masterson continued on this track throughout the 90s and, most recently, appeared with Delroy Lindo in Michael Miner's *The Book of Stars* (1999), a film which has yet to get a full theatrical release. She also appeared in the television movie *Black and Blue* (1999) and is set to write and direct her own film called *Grapefruit Moon* (2000).

TIM ROBBINS
Born 16 October 1958
New York City

This 6'5", baby-faced actor went from small roles in teen movies of the 80s to become a critically acclaimed movie star, playwright and director by the early 90s. Pauline Kael of *The New York Times* wrote: "He has the gift of looking just right for each of his roles, and has a Puckish, commanding presence… He makes you feel that behind his sneaky, demon eyes he's thinking thoughts no character in a movie ever thought before."

Tim Robbins grew up in New York. The son of a Grennwich Village folk singer, his father Gil was a member of The Highwaymen, who had a number one hit record *Michael Row the Boat Ashore*. By the age of 12, Robbins junior was already acting in school plays and later in experimental street theatre in different parts of the city. While attending New York University, he worked as a lighting technician at an off-Broadway theatre before later moving to Los Angeles, where he joined the UCLA theatre programme. After graduating with honours, he went on to study with the French actor George Bigot of the Theatre Du Soleil. He then formed the Actors' Gang with a bunch of like-minded friends in 1981. It quickly became one of Los Angeles' top theatre companies: "We wanted to do Surrealism, German Expressionism, a lot of strange shit. Anyway, not musicals or classical re-hashes. We combined the discipline of Shakespeare with the variety of rock 'n' roll," he explains.

Robbins took a hands-on role in the Gang, writing, directing and helping get productions financed. At the same time, the young actor was finding work in various television movies and series including *Hill Street Blues* and *St Elsewhere*. Later, at the age of 26, Robbins landed a part in *Toy Soldiers* (1984) as one of a group of college kids who try to rescue their friends from kidnappers in Central America. Another small role followed in *No Small Affair* (1984), a coming-of-age romance starring Demi Moore and Jon Cryer. But if you blink, you'll miss this brief appearance by Robbins.

It was the actor's next role that got him noticed, in Rob Reiner's teen romance *The Sure Thing* (1985). The lead roles of Gib and Alison went to John Cusack and Daphne

Zuniga, although Robbins as Gary Cooper – "But not the Gary Cooper that's dead" – and Lisa Jane Persky as Mary Anne Webster shine as a happy couple who drive them to California. "You guys know any show tunes?" asks Gary before he and Mary Anne burst into *The Age of Aquarius*. But then things turn sour. On the cross country trip, Alison pulls off her bra to flash a truck driver. As a result, Gary, as the owner of the car, is charged with indecent exposure and reckless driving. He throws out Gib and Alison's luggage and drives off, leaving them stranded.

After the success of *The Sure Thing*, Robbins took a role in a cheesy teen sex comedy, *Fraternity Vacation* (1985), which mixed Florida sunshine with all-American teens, beer and bikini contests. Robbins played Mother, a leader of one of two rival frat groups desperate to impress the foxiest gal in Palm Springs, ex-Dallas star Sheree J Wilson. But even worse was to come when Robbins starred in *Howard the Duck* (1986), a disastrous adaptation of a comic-book character, which was described by critics as one of the worst films ever made. However, Robbins was also in the biggest hit of 1986, *Top Gun*, as Merlin, one of Tom Cruise's co-pilots, although at least the film about the cute duck wasn't an outrageously pro-war movie which made shooting down enemy aircraft look cool. Not surprising, after his involvement with such films, Robbins took time out. After two years off-screen, he made a comeback in a film set in the Bronx, about the 1964 civil rights movement, playing Harry, an Irish working-class kid with a conscience. The film's other stars were Jodie Foster and John Turturro. More of a critical than commercial success. Next, Robbins teamed up with his pal John Cusack for Bill Fishman's *Tapeheads* (1988), a comedy about two wannabe rock video directors. Robbins played Josh Tager, an expert in the field of electronics, even though he's clumsy with everything else. As the Video Aces, the dynamic duo are hired to produce a live televised concert by "Menudo", which is to be watched by 30 million people around the world. "Let's get into trouble, baby!"

Robbins then became the baseball pitcher with a 'megaton throw', Ebby Calvin 'Nuke' Laloosh in Ron Shelton's *Bull Durham* (1988). Susan Sarandon was the all-time baseball groupie, who selects one player each season to receive her own special brand of erotic instruction – in this case Robbins. The film enabled him to show off both his comic and dramatic skills. Sarandon, 12 years his senior, later became Robbins' wife and mother to his two son's Jack Henry and Miles Guthrie.

Robbins' comic talents were needed again for the Deep South comedy drama, *Miss Firecracker* (1989), an adaptation of Beth Henley's play about a small town Mississippi beauty pageant, in which he played local loony toon Delmont 'Jughead' Williams. Robbins landed the title role in Terry Jones' Pythonesque *Erik the Viking* (1989), but the flat jokes and cheap special effects resulted in empty theatres.

Staying with comedy roles, Robbins then proved more than an adequate match for Robin 'Please Love Me' Williams in *Cadillac Man* (1990) as a crazed gunman who storms a showroom and holds customers hostage. But the film was overlong and not that funny at all, come to think of it.

Robbins then returned to serious drama as a Vietnam veteran suffering hallucinations in Adrian Lyne's *Jacob's Ladder* (1990). Critically acclaimed as an innovative piece of film-making, audiences were simply confused by the abstract style. It was not a success.

However, 1992 was a great year for Robbins. He starred in Robert Altman's *The Player* and walked away with the Best Actor award at that year's Cannes Film Festival. In Altman's send-up of Hollywood, Robbins was top studio executive Griffin Mill, whose latest movies are flops, resulting in rumours he's about to be replaced by a rival suit. Still man of the moment after the 92 Cannes festival, Robbins released his own directorial debut, *Bob Roberts* (1992), a political satire set in the 1960s. In this documentary spoof, Robbins takes the title role as the millionaire and music-maker turned Senate candidate, who uses his charm and power to dislodge his political opponent. As well as starring and directing, Robbins wrote the music and sang the songs.

Himself a powerful name in Hollywood, Robbins used this success to attract money for his own projects such as *Dead Man Walking* (1995), which he directed. The story of the friendship between a New Orleans nun (Susan Sarandon) and a convicted killer (Sean Penn), Robbins' film won the Best Actress Oscar for Sarandon. Robbins has also been courted by a long list of high-calibre directors, including the Coen Brothers for *The Hudsucker Proxy* (1994) and he's continued to work with Robert Altman – *Short Cuts* (1993) and *Pret-a-Porter* [US: *Ready to Wear*] (1994). More recently, Robbins appeared in Brian De Palma's *Mission to Mars* (2000), a film which should have carried the tagline, "In space, no one can hear you scream … with boredom."

MICKEY ROURKE
(Philip Rourke)
Born 16 September 1953
Schenectady, New York

Many of Mickey Rourke's films have achieved cult status, but they rarely pulled in the crowds. He's always had a reputation for being difficult to work with and yet has, until recently, had directors queuing up. He has a devoted band of followers and is an icon in France, having become a sex symbol without possessing the standard Hollywood Brat Pack looks (clean cut with perfect teeth). Rourke can be admired for turning down Hollywood meatball movies such as *Beverly Hills Cop* and *Top Gun*, preferring to take on roles in more interesting, smaller films such as his sixth-billing in Nicolas Roeg's 1982 film *Eureka*.

Born Philip but nicknamed Mickey (after the mouse), Rourke grew up in the tough neighbourhoods of Miami and then New York. Originally, he was set to become a boxer, but a chance invitation to act in a college production of Genet's *Deathwatch* changed his mind. In New York, he joined the Method-based Actor's Studio and earned money by working in massage parlours and brothels – a past he's no doubt used in a string of dark, unpleasant acting roles.

After moving to Los Angeles, Rourke got work in various television movies, but a cameo in Steven Spielberg's *1941* was his big break. A small role in *Fade to Black* followed, as well as a part in Michael Cimino's *Heaven's Gate* (he was Christopher Walken's henchman), but Rourke had more to do in Lawrence Kasdan's *Body Heat* (1981), in which he played an intense explosives expert to whom struggling lawyer William Hurt turns for advice on arson and murder.

Rourke brought an air of knowing calm to films packed with clean cut brats. Essentially, he was one of the Brats, but always the 'bit of rough' in the Pack. His use of stillness and tone of voice set him apart from the rest in both *Diner* and *Rumble Fish*. In Barry Levinson's directorial debut *Diner* (1982), a group of guys (including Steve Guttenberg, Daniel Stern and Kevin Bacon) meet at a drab diner in Baltimore to talk about how good their Friday night dates were. Rourke was impressive as the womanising hairdresser Boogie, the sauve Don Juan of the group who would seduce women by pretending he was a law student. But his finest hour was in Francis Ford Coppola's *Rumble Fish* (1983), the story of a young punk (Matt Dillon) who idolises his older brother, a gang leader known as 'The Motorcycle Boy' (Rourke). A hero not just to his brother but to a whole neighbourhood, Rourke's ageing idol character is completely hip. In fact, Coppola's seminal film has an impressive line-up of American teenage stars acting their hearts out like there was no tomorrow. Unfortunately, for Rourke, there wasn't – he has never bettered his role as the eccentric Motorcycle Boy.

Nevertheless, Rourke is probably best remembered for his role in Adrian Lyne's supposedly 'erotic' movie *9½ Weeks*. He is not at all convincing as a Wall Street executive who indulges in an intense love affair with a beautiful art gallery entrepreneur played by Kim Basinger. The film bombed in America, but was a big hit in Europe. Basinger later dubbed Rourke "The Human Ashtray".

Rourke was earning a lot of money, but also spending it too: "I guess I earned more than most people make in a lifetime," he admits. "Spent it foolishly. When you get your hands on money for the first time in your life, you don't keep it in your pocket. I regret that I was so reckless with it, but that goes along with a lot of other things in my life that I lost along the way through that kind of behaviour."

Throughout the 80s, Rourke continued to play unshaven loners and tough guys, characters who seem to be just about coping with all sorts of pressures – notably the hard-boiled detective Stanley White in Cimino's *Year of the Dragon* (1985), a violent and dynamic drama perfect for Rourke's offbeat screen persona. The same can be said for Alan Parker's *Angel Heart* (1987) in which Rourke is the private-eye Harry Angel, hired by the mysterious Louise Cyphre (Robert De Niro) to find a former crooner from the pre-war days who, according to De Niro, failed to live up to the terms of a contract. His search takes him into the dark world of the occult and his leads all wind up dead in a series of ritual murders. Once again, Rourke gets his kit off – this time for a sex scene with former Cosby kid Lisa Bonnet, who plays the poor black girl from Louisiana voodoo country. The bizarre sequence involves blood spilling down on the pair from leaks in the ceiling, intercut with glimpses of strange voodoo rituals. The scene was cut in the US to avoid an X certificate.

In *A Prayer for the Dying* (1987), as a disillusioned, mumbling assassin, the Rourkster was undoubtedly the least realistic Oirishman in cinema history; while the semi-autobiographical *Homeboy* (1989), which had Rourke as a small town boxer, went straight to video in America. Rourke had spent nine years perfecting the script and did the fight scenes himself. His subsequent attempt in 1991 to make a real professional boxing comeback only earned him more derision.

Rourke failed to turn on a mass audience with *Wild Orchid* (1990), which saw him back as a wealthy seducer taking his then real-life wife Carré Otis to the limit of her desires; and the obscure thriller *White Sands* (1992) was equally as unsuccessful. Rourke also attempted to change his image slightly in the hell-for-leather comedy-adventure *Harley Davidson and the Marlboro Man* (1991), which according to studio press releases "showed the lighter side of Mickey Rourke". However, as the former rodeo cowboy, he barely manages a grin, let alone a smile.

Things went from bad to worse for Rourke as the 90s progressed. In July 1994, he was arrested by the LAPD and charged with spousal abuse. It was therefore no surprise when his marriage to Carré Otis ended in divorce a few months later. His role in the long-awaited Terrence Malick comeback film *The Thin Red Line* (1998) ended up on the cutting room floor and in August 1999, to crown an impossibly pitiful career, Rourke walked off the set of *Luck of the Draw* when the producers refused to let him include his pet Chihuahua in the movie.

Despite such incidents, Rourke believes he is now a born-again actor: "I'm starting over, in a way. About 10 years ago I had my career going in the right direction. Then I started not liking the business and not liking myself. And I was slowly self-destructing, at a pretty fast rate – if that makes sense. I got to the point where I was hanging around with an element I probably shouldn't have been. But I felt comfortable in that element. I felt like I didn't belong in acting – I felt some sort of guilt about being successful at it. Being an actor is what I now call behaving in a professional manner – being responsible and consistent, not just hour by hour, day by day, or night by night, but all the way through. That was what I found most difficult. Let's say, if a little wrench got thrown in my spokes, I went haywire. And I was very consistent with my anger."

Rourke has never been interested in 'bankability': "I've watched actors I've admired over the years sell-out. That's the worst crime of all." However, despite managing to retain the air of an outsider, by the end of the 1990s, Rourke seemed in danger of disappearing altogether.

JAMES SPADER
Born 7 February 1960
Boston, Massachusetts

Although James Spader is probably best known for his role as the lonely yuppie voyeur in *Sex, Lies and Videotape* (1989), he had already proved a skilful actor before this breakthrough role – usually characterised as the white, middle-class snob. He shone in this bad-guy guise in both *Pretty in Pink* (1986) and *Less Than Zero* (1987).

The son of teachers Todd and Jean Spader, James attended the elite Phillips Academy in Andover, but later dropped out in the 11th grade. He moved to New York to study acting at the Michael Chekhov Studio and supported himself by waiting tables, teaching yoga and shovelling manure. It was at a health club in New York where he met a fellow yoga instructor, Victoria Kheel, whom he married eight years later. They have two children: Sebastian and Elijah.

Spader's official biog would have us believe that his movie debut was in Franco Zeffirelli's *Endless Love* (1981), a film derided by critics and mainly ignored by audiences. It is true he did have a small part to play in that film (as Brooke Shields' brother), but it was most certainly not his debut film performance. 'Jimmy' Spader had previously appeared as the town drunk in a soft-core 70s porno feature called *Team-Mates* (1978). Interestingly, Tom Cruise did make his debut in Zeffirelli's *Endless Love* and was billed eleven places below Spader.

After the Zeffirelli film was received so badly, Spader spent a while in the world of television movies – with typical made-for-television titles: *Cocaine: One Man's Seduction* (1983) and *A Killer in the Family* (1983). In the latter, he and Eric Stoltz played Robert Mitchum's sons who are talked into breaking him and a pal out of prison. The two became good buddies and were later paired up again for Sean S Cunningham's thriller *The New Kids* (1985). During this time, Spader had taken to driving across the States for weeks at a time in his classic Porsche sports car. Stoltz was always the passenger: "We'd take road trips to the Keys or up the coast, and he'd insist on having weapons in the trunk. He'd drive like a maniac – fast, with the music blaring – and I was always in fear that we'd be pulled over and some officer would find his crossbows, his lance, his 12-inch knife, his whip… He's the sweetest, nicest man in the world. He's just a tad eccentric."

Spader was caught breaking the speed limit more than once, although it wasn't just bouts of crazy driving. He fully immersed himself in the Hollywood high life of actors' parties, strip clubs and drinking sessions. Meanwhile, Spader landed his first lead role in *Tuff Turf* (1985) as a cute teenager from the East who has trouble adjusting to an inner-city California high school. The film was no more than a routine teen tale and meant Spader was reduced to fifth billing in his next outing, as Andrew McCarthy's snobby, cruel, rich-kid friend Steff in the John Hughes-scripted classic Brat Pack movie, *Pretty in Pink* (1986). Every word he uttered oozed venom, as he constantly mocked McCarthy's relationship with poor kid Molly Ringwald: "My best friend's conversing with a mutant," he smarms. "You really don't think she's got something?" asks McCarthy's Blane. "No, I really don't," replies an icy cold Steff, who also manages to confront Ringwald's Andie. Leaning against her banger of a car, he stares at her: "Andie, you look ravishing," he sneers. As she drives off, he calls out: "I'd go and see a doctor 'cause that condition of yours could get a lot worse." However, Steff eventually gets his comeuppance when, in the final prom scene, Blane turns on him: "You buy everything, Steff, but you couldn't buy her and that's what's killing you… She thinks you're shit and deep down you know she's right." Blane walks away from the gob-smacked Steff and apologises to Andie.

Pretty in Pink was a big hit and offers began pouring in for Spader. He chose to play a department store executive (again opposite Andrew McCarthy) in *Mannequin* (1987), but regretted it: "It was like some medieval torture sitting through that film," he admitted later. Next, Spader played the ultimate Yuppie as Diane Keaton's young assistant in *Baby Boom* (1987), a role which turned out to be simply preparation for a more serious project, Oliver Stone's *Wall Street* (1987), in which Spader again played a cut-throat yuppie type who takes to insider trading. In the same year, he appeared in *Less Than Zero*, as a businessman-like drug dealer.

Just the one movie for Spader in 1988: *Jack's Back,* a dual role as a young man who becomes involved in the case of a modern Jack the Ripper, this time killing on the streets of Los Angeles rather than London. Then came Spader's breakthrough role as Graham, the lonely and impotent voyeur in Steven Soderbergh's low-budget first film, *Sex, Lies and Videotape* (1989). Spader's character gets his kicks from making taped interviews of women's sexual experiences, but then finds it hard not to be involved when his latest subject is his best friend's wife. His intense and creepily menacing performance won him the Best Actor prize at the Cannes film festival, while the film itself (shot on location in Baton Rouge on a shoestring budget of $1.2 million) became a sleeper hit and won the coveted Palm D'Or.

Yet another yuppie role came along in 1990: in *White Palace* Spader starred as a young businessman who's seduced by Susan Sarandon's older sexy, working class waitress. The film is rather like *The Graduate* and Spader's advertising executive is a bit like a more mature version of his *Pretty in Pink* character. Next, Spader played opposite John Cusack in *True Colours* (1991) as an idealistic lawyer seeking truth and justice. A cameo as a newsreader in Tim Robbins' *Bob Roberts* (1992) followed.

Throughout the 90s, Spader slowly managed to work his way up the Hollywood ladder. He appeared with Jack Nicholson and Michelle Pfieffer in Mike Nichols' *Wolf* (1994) and starred as Dr Daniel Jackson in the unexpected hit sci-fi fantasy *Stargate* (1994). This led to a lead role in David Cronenberg's *Crash* (1996), in which he starred as James Ballard, who's drawn into a world where sexual kicks come from twisted metal, chrome and blood-stained dashboards. The crazed cross-country trips with Stoltz in the 80s suddenly spring to mind, although Cronenberg was surprised at how eager Spader was to play the role: "It was obvious he wasn't afraid to play unromantic or strange characters. But I didn't realise the depths to which he was willing to go in terms of exploring the dark. He really was an incredible collaborator and buddy once we started. He said that he was afraid of the script, as well as being intrigued, terrified and mystified by it. But he absolutely wanted to do it. So I thought, 'He's my kind of guy.' He did want to know who else was going to be in *Crash*, because he said, 'After all, I do fuck everybody in the movie.' So I thought, 'He's going to be fine.' And by God he was more than fine."

By the late 90s and into the new millennium, Spader had undoubtedly secured his status as one of the quality actors of his generation. Not bad for a guy who started out in a cheapie 70s porn flick.

ERIC STOLTZ
Born 30 September 1961
American Samoa (South Pacific)

Although he didn't have a big part to play in any of the classic Brat Pack movies, Eric Stoltz makes it as a hanger-on because of his brief appearance in Amy Heckerling's spirited high-school comedy, *Fast Times at Ridgemont High* (1982), his starring role in the John Hughes teen romance *Some Kind of Wonderful* (1987) – and for dating Ally Sheedy for five years.

The slim, red-headed, versatile actor was born in American Samoa, the son of two music teachers, although by the time he was eight, the family had moved four times – to Paris, then London, then New York, before finally settling in Santa Barbara. Stoltz began acting at school, appearing in theatrical productions and musicals. He studied theatre arts at USC, but dropped out to train with the legendary acting coach Peggy Feury. He later travelled to Europe and spent a season with an American rep company in Edinburgh.

Shortly after returning to the States, Stoltz began taking minor roles in television series (*The Violation of Sara McDavid* and *Paper Dolls*). Then, in 1982, he landed his first film role, as Stoner Bud, Sean Penn's surfer pal in *Fast Times at Ridgemont High*. A look at life in a Californian high school, based on Cameron Crowe's factual book, Amy Heckerling's film purported to "tell it like it is" and succeeded in becoming known as a key entry in the youth movie genre. The film also launched the careers of Jennifer Jason Leigh, Phoebe Cates and Anthony Edwards. After seeing Stoltz's brief appearance, Cameron Crowe promised him a role, however small, in every film he makes.

The success of *Fast Times* led to Art Linson's semi-sequel *The Wild Life* (1984), also scripted by Cameron Crowe. Stoltz played a similar character to Judge Reinhold's Brad – a wise guy, this time just out of high school, who's success falls through as soon as he moves into his bachelor pad. No Sean Penn, but brother Chris is there, in a similar key role as a stoned surfer.

A feeble follow-up to *Fast Times*, *The Wild Life* nevertheless convinced Robert

Zemeckis to cast Stoltz as Marty McFly in *Back to the Future* (1985), but just a few weeks into shooting he was fired and replaced by Michael J Fox. This was not as a result of on-set tantrums or rows but, according to Zemeckis, because Stoltz simply didn't act enough like a teenager: "I found myself with a very good actor playing the wrong part," declared the director.

Unfortunately, as the Stoltz-free *Back to the Future* was on its way to becoming one of the biggest grossing comedies ever, Stoltz had reverted back to his guise as a stoned surfer in a sophomoric movie called *Surf II* (1984) – even though *Surf I* didn't exist. It wasn't until he was cast in Peter Bogdanovich's Oscar-nominated *Mask* (1985) that people started to take Stoltz seriously. The film starred Cher as a hard-living, drug-taking biker and Stoltz as Rocky Dennis, her 16-year-old son who suffers from a disease which hideously deforms his face, inflating it to twice its normal size. Only his eyes were visible behind the amazing make-up job, but Stoltz gave a fine performance and won some great reviews.

Then it was back to teen angst in the John Hughes-scripted *Some Kind of Wonderful* (1987), although it was all some kind of familiar in terms of plot – Hughes had simply reworked his successful teen romance *Pretty in Pink* (1986). Here though, Stoltz was the poor male ignoring his tomboy friend in favour of a beautiful rich girl (Lea Thompson).

In 1988, Stoltz made his Broadway debut in a revival of Thornton Wilder's *Our Town* and earned Tony and Drama Desk nominations as a result. A couple of minor roles followed before Stoltz teamed up with John Cusack for *Say Anything* (1989), Cameron Crowe's acclaimed teen comedy, in which he got to dress up as a rooster to host a wild graduation party!

A change of direction followed, with Stoltz taking the lead in the horror movie *The Fly II* (1989), as the son of the original 'fly', Seth Brundle (Jeff Goldblum). Having inherited his genius, he continues to work on the teleportation machine, but being afflicted with the dramatically accelerated lifecycle of a fly, he begins to mutate into a beast while retaining his human feelings. Amid all the goo and gore, Stoltz is at home with the dark humour: "I was attracted to the fact that my character gradually becomes an insect," he said. "I prepared for the role by watching a lot of television specials, like *Life on Earth* and *National Geographic*."

Next, he co-starred with Mathew Modine, Sean Astin, Billy Zane and Harry Connick Jr in David Puttnam's sentimental and cliché-ridden wartime pic *Memphis Belle* (1990): he played Danny Daly, a World War Two radio operator on board a B-17 bomber. Later, Stoltz starred as paraplegic writer Joel Garcia in *The Waterdance* (1992), another role which won him good reviews. The following year, he got to produce his own film, *Bodies, Rest and Motion* (1993), which starred his long-term girlfriend, Bridget Fonda. Stoltz also starred in his film, turning in a funny performance as a painter who comforts Fonda after she's been dumped by boyfriend Tim Roth.

Originally conceived as a film-school project, Dan Algrant's *Naked in New York* (1994) was eventually executive-produced by Martin Scorsese and starred Stoltz as Jake, a Jewish neurotic in a uneasy relationship with Mary-Louise Parker. The story revolves around this relationship as well as Jake's dreams of success as a playwright.

Stoltz continued to get involved in more cool indie projects throughout the 90s – a cameo (again with Fonda) in *Singles* (1993), a part as a safecracker in the violent thriller *Killing Zoe* (1994, his role as Lance, the drug-supplier in Quentin Tarantino's arty action pic *Pulp Fiction* (1994) and a cameo in Cameron Crowe's *Jerry Maguire* (1996).

It is impossible to categorise Eric Stoltz. Whether it's top-billing or eighth-credited, he continues to appear across a variety of genres in a variety of different parts. He's always been this way and there's no doubt his attitude makes him all the more interesting and unusual for a Hollywood actor : "I have absolutely no agenda," he admits. "I have no career plan. I take what comes my way and what I think is interesting."

PATRICK SWAYZE
Born 18 August 1952
Houston, Texas

P atrick Swayze secured his place in the Brat Pack with appearances in *The Outsiders* as Rob Lowe and C Thomas Howell's older brother; *Grandview, USA*; *Red Dawn;* and *Youngblood*.

Swayze is an all-American good ole boy from Texas – and he's good at everything he does. He was a football star in his youth and went to university on a gymnastics scholarship. Trained by his dancer–choreographer mother Patsy, he spent time at two of America's top ballet companies – the Harkess Ballet School and the Joffrey – and was a principle dancer in the Eliot Field company. Besides being a silver-screen hunk of the 80s, he also became a proficient archer, carpenter, playwright, stuntman and martial artist. Swayze has also had, among other achievements, a Top 10 hit with a single from *Dirty Dancing*.

Sick of being bullied for his love of ballet, Swayze gave it all up for a while – to concentrate on athletics. Again, he was successful in his chosen route, but after making his professional debut as Prince Charming in *Disney On Parade,* he decided to take up dancing again as a full time career. Swayze moved to New York and won dancing roles on various productions. However, an old knee injury came back to haunt him and led to Swayze taking up acting rather than dancing.

After a successful few months as Danny in the long-running musical *Grease*, he moved to LA to further his acting career. He made his film debut with a small role as Ace, alongside Scott Biao, in the boring roller disco saga *Skatetown USA* (1979). Before his next movie part came along, Swayze played a mix of teenagers and tough guys on television, including a role as a brave young soldier dying of leukaemia in *M.A.S.H.*, a role which got Hollywood interested again…

Francis Ford Coppola signed up Swayze for the role of Darry Curtis in *The Outsiders* (1983), the film which became synonymous with the birth of the Brat Pack and the film which attracted a huge cult following. Darry was the oldest brother to C Thomas Howell, a kind of parental role with scenes of real emotion. Coppola's film became a showcase for a group of up-and-coming stars and, for the rest of the 80s, it would only be fellow *Outsider* Tom Cruise who would become a bigger star than Swayze. But for a while after the release of *The Outsiders*, it seemed all Swayze could get was a succession of uninteresting macho roles. He became more famous via the television mini-series *North and South* and the sequel *North and South Book II* in which he played Orry Main, an heroic officer who cut a fine dash in uniform.

"Food riots in Poland. El Salvador fails. Greens control Germany and demand end to nuclear arms in Europe. Mexican revolt. The US stands alone.": in 1984, Swayze was top-billed in the controversial *Red Dawn*, a film by John Milius which was based on the idea that some time in the future, as the United States stands alone and vulnerable to attack, the country is invaded by Cuban and Nicaraguan paratroopers. As Jed, Swayze leads a group of teenage vigilantes to the hills, where they successfully carry out raids on the invading army. The other teenagers included C Thomas Howell and Charlie Sheen. Unfortunately, all the film was really about was the expression of right-wing, gung-ho American patriotism with scenes that included Jed making a man of wimpy Howell by killing a deer and forcing him to drink the blood. Later in the year Swayze was back opposite C Thomas Howell in Randal Kleiser's *Grandview, USA* (1984), about a demolition derby in small-town America. Usual 80s pop soundtrack – lame plot. Swayze also assumed the role of choreographer on this movie.

In *Youngblood* (1986), Swayze was reunited with fellow *Outsider* Rob Lowe. Both played ice hockey players. Very lame. Very dull. But just when Swayze was in danger of bombing out, his star turn in *Dirty Dancing* (1987) brought him more success and fame than he could have ever imagined. Vestron, the company which had achieved overnight success with the marketing of videotapes, took its first major step into film production. The $5 million indie film became a smash hit and confirmed Swayze as Number One Hunk of 1987. He also received a Golden Globe nomination for Best Actor. Set in a Jewish Catskills vacation resort in the Sixties, the story revolved around two lovers from different backgrounds kept apart by the girl's meddling father. As resident dance instructor Johnny Castle, Swayze was like a modern Gene Kelly with a mix of nostalgic and trendier dance routines up his sleeve. Frances 'Baby' Houseman (Jennifer Grey) is the naïve young holidaymaker who falls for him. However, essentially a vehicle for Swayze to show off his physique, the film was, in the end, nothing more than clichéd melodrama where everyone had the time of their lives. On its release, Swayze was US stud of the month, having at one point to contend with 300 screaming women who'd discovered the whereabouts of his hotel: "Just as they smashed down my door, I dived off the balcony from the third floor into the shallow end of a swimming pool," he recalls. "I tell you, it was a narrow escape. Mass hysteria isn't a pretty sight, especially when it's your body they all want."

Offers were pouring in for Swayze – including a project called *Total Recall,* which he signed for. It fell through, before reappearing years later with Arnold Schwarzenegger attached. His next few films – the futuristic action movie *Steel Dawn* (1987), *Tiger Warsaw* (1988) and *Next of Kin* (1988) – all flopped. Swayze went from Dirty Dancing to Dirty Harry with the ultra-violent *Roadhouse* (1989), in which he played a bouncer at a rowdy Missouri bar. But it was becoming clear that Swayze had no base of fans within this genre – he simply couldn't compete with Schwarzenegger, Stallone and Willis. His own fans were women. No surprise then when his next film was a success.

In Jerry Zucker's unashamedly sentimental *Ghost* (1990), Swayze starred as a Wall Street whizz-kid who returns as a ghost to hunt down his killers. Demi Moore played his loving wife/widow. Swayze returns via medium Oda Mae Brown (Whoopi Goldberg), whom he asks to reassure his beloved Molly of his undying love. Sex, romance, bullets, *Ghost* had it all – including Swayze's naked chest, an Oscar for Goldberg and the infamous clay-moulding scene which must have given a huge boost in numbers applying for night-school pottery classes. Anyway, Swayze was back on track and, having bared his chest again, the film took over $200 million at the US box office (over $500 million globally). Co-star Moore had this to say of Swayze: "He brought a tremendous sensitivity and a vulnerability to the role. I don't know if there is anybody else who could have done it." On top of all that praise, as well as receiving another Golden Globe nomination, Swayze was voted one of the 50 most beautiful people in the world by *People* magazine in 1991.

He'd already signed for *Point Break* (1991) when the success of Ghost materialised. Playing opposite Keanu Reeves' FBI agent, Swayze was an elusive bank robber, with both finding themselves riding the wave. The film was another hit. Then, in Roland Joffe's *City of Joy* (1992), Swayze played American doctor Max Lowe trying to find meaning to his life while slumming it in Calcutta. "I would have done *City of Joy* for nothing. I would have paid them to do the movie," he said.

For the rest of the 90s, however, Swayze had to resign himself to a string of straight-to-video flops – *Tall Tale* (1993), *Father Hood* (1993) and *Three Wishes* (1995). The only interesting (and successful) film role he took in the 90s was as Vida Boheme, a gay transvestite with a heart of gold, in the camp comedy *To Wong Foo, Thanks For Everything! Julie Newmar* (1995). Co-starring with Wesley Snipes and John Leguizamo as a trio of street-wise cross-dressers in the Midwest, Swayze gave the most understated performance in what was essentially an outrageous romp. Initially, he'd had to fight very hard for the role: "I couldn't get seen because they had this picture of me that I was seriously, terribly macho and heterosexual. But I could not have had a hope of pulling off Miss Vida if I had a problem with my masculinity or who I was as a person. But as soon as I read the script I realised she's a fantasy; she's the dream of a human being. However, I kept coming back to the realisation that I had to make her real, I had to stop playing a man in a dress and see if I could create a woman."

Unfortunately, a year earlier, a classier trio were camping it up in *The Adventures of Priscilla, Queen of the Desert*, a film in which the glitz and glamour seemed far more stylish – less Hollywood and more believable to a gay audience.

Since his role as Miss Vida, Swayze has been involved in a few films which never really got off the ground and from 1998 was reduced to guesting on the US television quiz show *Hollywood Squares*. Nevertheless, he's content to sit and wait for the right part to come along: "I've now gotten to a place – having lived through the craziness of the career – where I'm not interested in the fame. I just want to see if I can be the best possible actor I can be."

DAPHNE ZUNIGA
Born 23 October 1963
Berkeley, California

In 1982, a young Daphne Zuniga appeared (albeit very briefly) in *The Dorm that Dripped Blood*, a run-of-the-mill teen thriller in which a group of youngsters are bumped off, one by one, by a mysterious killer. At the time, Zuniga was still at college and a very impressive student. But after landing her first bit-part, the 19-year-old wasn't interested in getting lost in academia. At 21, she was spotted by a talent scout whose interest resulted in Zuniga ditching a promising 'normal' career.

Early on in her acting career, the decision certainly seemed to have paid off. After another average teen campus thriller called *The Initiation* (1984) – based around a crazed psycho bumping off a bunch of college kids – Zuniga landed a role in *Vision Quest* aka *Crazy for You* (1985). It was a small part, but Harold Becker's film was a mainstream affair which starred both Matthew Modine and Madonna. As a result, Zuniga was spotted by Rob Reiner.

Reiner had just scored with his cult spoof rock documentary *This is Spinal Tap* (1984) and was in the process of casting his next film *The Sure Thing* (1985). He paired Zuniga up with John Cusack as two college students forced together on a cross-country trip from New England to Los Angeles. Cusack is Walter "Gib" Gibson, the wild, reckless student who lives life on the edge, while Zuniga is quiet and sensitive as Alison Bradbury, so much so in fact that she's advised by her English teacher Mrs. Taub to "loosen up". "Sleep when you feel like it, not when you think you should," laughs the professor. "Eat food that is bad for you at least once in a while. Have conversations with people whose clothes are not colour co-ordinated. Make love in a hammock."

Along the way, the couple get help from Tim Robbins and Lisa Jane Persky (as Gary and Mary Anne), who do little to change the awkward atmosphere between the unlikely couple. But Gib and Alison eventually find opposites really do attract and that together, they are 'the sure thing'. Zuniga was impressive in the duo, an equal match for co-star Cusack. Reiner's film was regarded by many as one of the better teen films of the 80s.

Next, Zuniga took a lead role in *Modern Girls* (1986) with other young actresses Cynthia Gibb and Virginia Madsen. The movie, about three girls out on the pull in the LA punk scene, was a total disaster and failed to get distribution beyond a few big cities in the US. A year later, Zuniga signed up for Mel Brooks' Star Wars spoof *Spaceballs* (1987), in which she appeared amid the puns and in-jokes as the Royally Spoiled Princess (the Princess Leia character). But the parody came 10 years too late and Zuniga's role as a Carrie Fisher clone did her no favours at all.

Having achieved most success as a strait-laced brain, Zuniga chose to rebel against this nice girl image by playing a Mexican hooker in *Last Rites* (1988), an interesting thriller in which she seduces a priest (Tom Berenger). As the beautiful femme fatale, Zuniga proved she could do serious drama. The scenes of her enjoying seedy sex should have given her a whole new image, but the film didn't make much impact.

Zuniga was then reunited with Matthew Modine in *Gross Anatomy* aka *A Cut Above* (1989), playing a medical student alongside Christine Lahti, Todd Field and John Scott Clough. Modine is trying to bluff his way through his studies with their help, much to the consternation of his tutors. The script is below average and although Zuniga does her best with it, her character just seems too one-dimensional. The filmed bombed because it was released at a time when people were becoming sick of endless innocuous medical-themed melodramas.

Zuniga then co-starred with Eric Stoltz in *The Fly II* (1989), the sequel to David Cronenberg's 1986 version of the camp classic. But Chris Walas' film tried too hard to rely on goo and gore to shock.

After working hard to gain a reputation as a talented, versatile actress, Zuniga never quite hit the bull's-eye in the 90s, with most of her films going straight to video – including *Mad at the Moon* (1992) and *Chameleon* (1993). She's guest-starred in a string of US television series, including *Spin City* (1996 – as Carrie) and *Batman Beyond* (1999 – as the voice of Lula); but Zuniga has been best known, in recent years, for her four-year stint as Jo on the American television series *Melrose Place*.

INDEX

About Last Night 47-51, 95
All the Right Moves 78

Bacon, Kevin 122-123, 143
Bad Boys 109, 110, 113
Bad Influence 81, 96
Beautiful Girls 82, 136
Breakfast Club, The 6, 7, 10, 11, 24, 31-37, 43, 44, 87, 88, 91, 92, 93, 107-107, 113
Brickman, Paul 78
Broderick, Matthew 23, 53, 74-76, 125

Carlino, John Lewis 94-5, 126
Class 18-21, 26, 94-95, 99, 126
Cocktail 78
Coppola, Francis Ford 8, 12, 14-15, 81, 131, 133, 144, 152
Cox, Alex 29-30, 81, 87-88, 128
Crowe, Cameron 9, 79, 82, 110, 127, 149
Cruise, Tom 7, 10, 21-22, 68, 77-79, 87, 101, 153
Cryer, Jon 74, 125, 140
Cusack, John 10, 25, 106, 126-128, 140, 147, 150, 155

De Mornay, Rebecca 21-22
Deutch, Howard 58, 100, 138
Dillon, Matt 7, 14, 67, 80-82, 100, 144
Diner 123, 143
Dirty Dancing 131-132, 152, 153
Downey Jr, Robert 54-56, 68, 83-86, 97, 129
Drugstore Cowboy 82

Endless Love 77, 129, 146
Estevez, Emilio 6, 10, 11, 12, 32, 37, 55, 63, 87-90, 92, 94, 96, 102, 116

Family Business 74, 76
Fast Times at Ridgemont High 9, 110, 149
Ferris Bueller's Day Off 52-53, 74-76, 116, 131
Fishman, Bill 127, 141
Footloose 124
Freshman, The 76
Fresh Horses 100, 105

Gertz, Jami 56, 84, 120, 129-130

Ghost 154

Glory 76

Grandview USA 126, 133, 152, 153

Grey, Jennifer 53, 75, 131-132, 152-153

Hall, Anthony Michael 25, 32, 43, 67, 84, 91-93, 99, 104, 113

Heaven Help Us 138

Hinton, SE 12, 29, 87, 89

Holland, Savage Steve 127

Howell, C Thomas 10, 12, 28, 77, 87, 133-134, 152, 153

Hughes, John 7, 24, 30, 34, 44, 53, 58-61, 88, 92, 93, 104, 105, 107, 113, 114, 124, 129, 131, 149, 150

Hutton, Timothy 7, 10, 77, 110, 135-137

Karate Kid, The 29, 97, 98

Legend 78

Less Than Zero 54-55, 84, 129,146, 147

Levinson, Barry 123, 143

Losin' It 77

Lost Boys, The 56-58, 129

Lowe, Rob 6, 10, 12, 19-21, 26, 37, 48-51, 66, 87, 94-96, 114, 116, 152

Macchio, Ralph 7, 12, 29, 67, 87, 97-98

MacDowal, Andie 37

Madonna 111, 155

Masterson, Mary Stuart 119, 138-139

McCarthy, Andrew 5, 6, 19-21, 26, 37, 44-47, 54, 55, 62, 67, 84, 95, 99-100, 122, 138, 147

Moore, Demi 6, 7, 38, 48-51, 55, 68, 74, 87, 89, 95, 103-105, 122, 125, 127, 140, 154

Nelson, Judd 6, 32, 37, 52, 55, 66, 94, 105, 106-108, 122

No Small Affair 74, 101, 125, 140

One Crazy Summer 127

Outsiders, The 12-15, 17, 29, 77, 81, 87, 133, 152

Over the Edge 80

Oxford Blues 26-27, 51, 95, 114

Penn, Sean 10, 67, 77, 109-112, 116, 119, 136, 138

Phoenix, River 120

Pick-Up Artist, The 84

Pretty in Pink 10, 24, 44-47, 100, 125, 146, 147, 150

Red Dawn 27-28

Repo Man 29-30, 87-88, 90

Ringwald, Molly 6, 32, 44-47, 56-7, 66, 84, 92, 93, 100, 104-105, 107, 113, 114

Risky Business 21-22, 24, 78

Robbins, Tim 127, 140-142, 155

Rourke, Mickey 123, 143-145

Rumble Fish 15, 17, 81, 144

Say Anything 127, 150

Sheedy, Ally 23, 26, 37, 52, 66, 92, 113-115, 149

Sheen, Charlie 7, 53, 88, 94, 116-118, 153

Schumacher, Joel 7, 38, 56, 58, 102, 120, 129

Singles 82

Sixteen Candles 25-26, 28, 30, 91, 104, 113, 129

Some Kind of Wonderful 58-61

Spader, James 45, 55, 146-148

St. Elmo's Fire 6, 7, 10, 31, 36-42, 51, 87, 89, 95, 99, 102, 107, 121

Stand By Me 52, 56, 119, 127

Stoltz, Eric 60, 61, 138, 146, 149-151

Sure Thing, The 126, 155

Sutherland, Kiefer 7, 56, 58, 66, 110, 119-120, 129

Swayze, Patrick 12, 87, 132, 133, 152-154

Tapeheads 127, 141

Taps 10, 77, 110

Tex 29, 81, 87

Top Gun 78

Walken, Christopher 76

Wargames 23, 74, 75, 113

Weird Science 42, 83, 93

Winningham, Mare 66, 121-122

Wisdom 89, 102

Youngblood 51-53

Young Guns 62, 90, 116, 118, 120

Zuniga, Daphne 126, 141, 155-156